LIFE IN THE FASD LANE

of related interest

We're All Neurodiverse
How to Build a Neurodiversity-Affirming Future
and Challenge Neuronormativity
Sonny Jane Wise
ISBN 978 1 83997 578 3
eISBN 978 1 83997 579 0
AUDIO ISBN 978 1 39981 636 6

The Pocket Guide to Neurodiversity
Daniel Aherne
Illustrated by Tim Stringer
ISBN 978 1 83997 014 6
eISBN 978 1 83997 015 3
AUDIO ISBN 978 1 39980 420 2

Notes for Neuro Navigators
The Allies' Quick-Start Guide to Championing Neurodivergent Brains
Jolene Stockman
ISBN 978 1 83997 868 5
eISBN 978 1 83997 869 2
AUDIO ISBN 978 1 39981 239 9

10 Minutes to Better Mental Health
A Step-by-Step Guide for Teens Using CBT and Mindfulness
Lee David and Debbie Brewin
Illustrated by Rebecca Price
ISBN 978 1 78775 556 7
eISBN 978 1 78775 570 3
AUDIO ISBN 978 1 39980 413 4

Understanding Fetal Alcohol Spectrum Disorder
A Guide to FASD for Parents, Carers and Professionals
Maria Catterick and Liam Curran
ISBN 978 1 84905 394 5
eISBN 978 0 85700 758 2
JKP ESSENTIALS

Life in the FASD Lane

Rossi's Fabulous Guide to Navigating Your Teens and Young Adulthood

Rossi Griffin

Foreword by Professor Raja Mukherjee
Illustrated by Tim Stringer

Jessica Kingsley Publishers
London and Philadelphia

First published in Great Britain in 2025 by Jessica Kingsley Publishers
An imprint of John Murray Press

1

Copyright © Rossino Griffin 2025

The right of Rossino Griffin to be identified as the Author of the Work has been asserted by him in accordance with the Copyright, Designs and Patents Act 1988.

Foreword © Raja Mukherjee 2025
An Editor's Tale © Mel Byron 2025
A Mum's Eye View © Janet Griffin 2025

All rights reserved. No part of this publication may be reproduced, stored in a retrieval system, or transmitted, in any form or by any means without the prior written permission of the publisher, nor be otherwise circulated in any form of binding or cover other than that in which it is published and without a similar condition being imposed on the subsequent purchaser.

A CIP catalogue record for this title is available from the British Library and the Library of Congress

ISBN 978 1 80501 418 8
eISBN 978 1 80501 419 5

Printed and bound in Great Britain by TJ Books

Jessica Kingsley Publishers' policy is to use papers that are natural, renewable and recyclable products and made from wood grown in sustainable forests. The logging and manufacturing processes are expected to conform to the environmental regulations of the country of origin.

Jessica Kingsley Publishers
Carmelite House
50 Victoria Embankment
London EC4Y 0DZ

www.jkp.com

John Murray Press
Part of Hodder & Stoughton Ltd
An Hachette Company

The authorised representative in the EEA is Hachette Ireland, 8 Castlecourt Centre, Dublin 15, D15 XTP3, Ireland (email: info@hbgi.ie)

Contents

Acknowledgements		7
Foreword by Professor Raja Mukherjee OBE		8
Prologue		11

1:	Introduction	14
2:	How to Read This Book	18
3:	What Is FASD?	20
4:	Neurotypical and Neurodivergent	23
5:	Growing Up	25
6:	Senior School	29
7:	A Little Extra Help: Ups, Downs and Medication	32
8:	Impulsive? Me?	35
9:	A Friendship Tale	39
10:	School Bullies	42
11:	A Clinic, a Doll's House and a Pointy Cup	44
12:	A Marble-ous Story	48
13:	Living With My Brain Now: Dichotomies	52
14:	Sleep	56
15:	Everybody Needs a Safe Space	59

16: A Literal Basket Case 62

17: The Best Form of Defence? 66

18: Focus, Focus 70

19: OCD, TAF: Scary Thoughts, an Elephant and Pizza 73

20: Distracted 78

21: Independence 82

22: Brain Domains 85

23: Adulting With a Puppy Brain 92

24: The Rock: Anxiety and Low Mood 97

25: A Pinch of Salt 101

26: Global Developmental Delay 104

27: Abstract Thinking 110

28: The Energy Bank 114

29: My Fabulous Umbrella 117

30: Hard Work 121

31: Alcohol and Me 125

32: *Mum's Eye View* 128
Jan, Rossi's mum

33: What Can We Do to Stop FASD? 133

34: Finding Our Brilliant 136

35: The Real Rossi – At Last 139

An Editor's Tale 142

Acknowledgements

Without my mum this book would no way be possible. Keeping me on track, pushing me (even when I didn't want to be pushed!). Thank you, Mum... For everything. More than this book. Thank you for making me me and insisting I be my best version. For teaching me to show kindness no matter what. For being there... Always.

Mel Byron... Editor in chief... You went on a learning curve you didn't sign up for...but you are a quick learner and FASD is not a quick learn. Thank you for being patient with me (and my mum while she pushed me!). Thank you because you are fabulous!

To all the FASD world... Me and my brain... Surrey FASD Clinic... Those who see me and my FASD but see first the abilities in disabilities. To all my friends across the world with FASD...keep being you, people...your FASD does not define you... it can be your superpower. And thank you for all your amazing support. Let's get the world listening.

Foreword

Professor Raja Mukherjee OBE

It was back in 2013 that I first met Rossi. Just over ten years later it is a pleasure and a delight to be asked to write the foreword for his book. Our first encounter was when he came to my clinic with his mother seeking a diagnosis. At that time our clinic was probably the only clinic in the UK that specialized in diagnosing fetal alcohol spectrum disorder (FASD).

FASD is a condition that causes damage to both body and brain, which can be attributed to the consumption of alcohol by the pregnant mother. In almost all cases any harm is unintentional, and while there may be regret and guilt felt, as has been shown here, dwelling on this is not always the most helpful situation. Instead, recognizing the issue, understanding how to get the best out of the individual and building on strengths as well as supporting any difficulties are the keys to long-term success. It was for this reason I was first introduced to Rossi. He and his mum Jan are a great example of learning, as a pair, how to maximize abilities and at the same time provide support where needed.

FASD is often a hidden condition. In most cases, the

individual does not look any different. While the most recognizable part of the spectrum of conditions are those where facial features exist, this is rare. Instead, most people only have the brain-related issues, with areas of strength and weakness. The weaknesses often revolve around planning, decision-making and memory, as well as in more severe cases, inattention and social communication difficulties. These can often be missed, and any behaviours that present as a result are often inappropriately labelled. It is only when recognizing how to support the individual long term that the best outcomes are achieved.

For Rossi, the journey has not been necessarily easy, but with the support of his mother and those around him, he is progressing really well. He has grown into an engaging, fun and caring individual. That is not to say he does not have his moments – just ask his mother – but he is an advocate for others and someone who demonstrates that by following their dreams, even despite having difficulties, positive outcomes can be reached.

A decade after I first met Rossi, we were re-acquainted in a different role and I have been able to get to know the adult, not just the child I met all those years ago. For much of his life, as he was growing up, he struggled with many issues. He was someone who did not know who he wanted to be, which proved a challenge for him and those around him. With the right support, however, he got through it. He continues to have a hidden problem and his superficial eloquence belies his need to seek help. Because Rossi has developed an understanding of his own condition, and those around him accommodate for this, it has meant that he is now undertaking work and studies in an area he excels at. You only have to look at the make-up artistry that he helped complete for charity to see his skill set.

Rossi has developed from an anxious child into an adult who has a place in society. Society will need to continue to recognize that Rossi needs support but, with a little bit of help on an ongoing basis, and a few reasonable adjustments, he can be a contributing member of society and is a wonderful person to spend time with.

It is only by seeing past the superficial and looking at the deeper person that the true Rossi is understood. He is a young man of complexity, as are so many, but while he acknowledges and understands his FASD, and remains an advocate for others, FASD does not define him.

First and foremost, he is an individual who is unique and a delight to know. I am sure he will continue to help shape FASD for adults in the UK due to his persistence and resilience. It will be a pleasure for me to continue to observe him, I hope, for many decades to come. I wish him well with this book and thank him for asking me to write this short foreword.

Prologue

December 2023.

I am working on hair and make-up on a professional photo shoot, when my phone rings. I have been waiting so long for this call.

'You should know it's been a very hard decision,' are the first words I hear. My heart sinks. They haven't chosen me.

'But,' she continues, 'we'd like to offer you a spot on *Glow Up*, season six.'

I am too stunned to speak. Eventually I say, 'Thank you so much. This means the world to me. I have to get back on the set now.'

Seriously, this is the biggest news of my life, and I have cut the poor woman off!

Glow Up is a BBC reality television series, in which a group of make-up artists compete against each other in a number of creative challenges. Each week, somebody is eliminated before eventually one of them is crowned the winner.

For a make-up artist, winning *Glow Up* can be life changing.

You can understand why, as someone breaking into the profession, I had applied to be on the show.

I had, of course, promised my mum that I would do no more television after my appearance on Channel 4's *First Dates*. My date was nice, but nothing came of it.

Even though I enjoyed the process of being on *First Dates*, it was stressful, for me and for my mum.

I have FASD and many everyday things are a struggle for me.

Doing *Glow Up* would be a huge upheaval. It would involve being away from home and being filmed for several weeks. For sure, there would be joyous high points, but there would also be tears.

I would also have to expend a lot of energy to focus and to be creative every single day – unless I got eliminated very early on. I didn't want that. This was too important.

But tears, there would be tears.

How would my FASD brain cope? Mum and I were soon to find out.

In the meantime, I had a contract with Jessica Kingsley Publishing, and I had a book to write.

Perhaps I had taken on too much.

CHAPTER 1

Introduction

This book shouldn't exist.

No, seriously.

It's not because the world doesn't need it. Believe me, we really need this book. Somebody had to write it. I decided that somebody should be me.

My name is Rossino Griffin, but please call me Rossi. I am 22 years old, and I have fetal alcohol spectrum disorder, or FASD.

This condition occurs when a baby is exposed to alcohol while in the womb. Put simply, if a pregnant woman drinks, for example, a glass of wine, the alcohol in the wine affects the development of the unborn child. This can cause a number of issues that affect both the brain and the body.

In all, researchers have identified over 420 conditions that can co-occur with FASD. Most of us, thankfully, do not have all of them, but many of us have more than one. Here is a list of just a few of the conditions that I live with: attention deficit hyperactivity disorder (ADHD), epilepsy, hypermobility, hypertension, memory deficit, anxiety disorder, autism spectrum disorder (ASD).

INTRODUCTION

This book shouldn't exist because of that first condition, ADHD. This causes difficulty with focus and attention. I really struggle to focus. My mind tends to wander off all over the place. It's hard to write a book when all you can think about is...well, anything, except writing a book.

Are you feeling as peckish as I am? I wonder what's for dinner. Maybe I'll get a takeaway.

I do find it hard to concentrate on one thing. Like this book. Or making a television programme like *Glow Up*. Or worse, trying to do both of those at once!

Chips would be good. Or a loaded baked potato.

Oh, wait, yes, the book.

So, how many people have FASD? It's hard to be exact. Some very clever people at Salford University recently did some research which suggested that around 3.6 per cent of children and young people in the UK have FASD. Other clever people at Bristol University have suggested that the figure might be as high as 17 per cent!

Right now, it's impossible to give an exact number. But we do know that many people may be living with the condition without even knowing it. This is causing stress to them and their families.

Then there's the stress, once you are diagnosed, of trying to live your life with the condition.

That's why I wanted to tell my story. You can read the research papers and learn about FASD. But what is it really like living with FASD day to day? I'll tell you in the coming chapters. I'll give you an insight into my life, which has sometimes been very difficult, and into some of the challenges that many of us living with FASD face on a regular basis.

When I was growing up, adults and other children around me thought my behaviour was odd, even irritating. Nobody understood me. I was struggling with everyday tasks and interactions. They said, 'Rossi's naughty' or, 'He just doesn't listen'.

I was 12 when I was eventually diagnosed with FASD. That was a real breakthrough, as it meant I could get the support I needed. My teaching assistant, Elle, had realized that the normal ASD strategies were not working for me and when the FASD diagnosis was given she quickly adapted her approach. This involved fewer words and overlearning. Getting diagnosed can be difficult because the behaviours are often similar to conditions such as autism and Asperger's syndrome.

At one point, when I was in primary school, my teachers thought I was deaf. I didn't follow the rules of 'normal' behaviour, so they assumed I couldn't hear them. You see, in addition to having trouble focusing, I can also come across as a bit rebellious, even rude. I'm not deaf, by the way, but I do have a slight hearing problem on my left side. Hearing impairment is also on that list of 420-plus conditions.

Perhaps what you've read so far is already a lot of new information. I'm not surprised. It's really only in the last ten years or so, thanks to the work of amazing people like the university professors who did the research I mentioned, that progress has been made in diagnosing FASD. With that has come progress in helping those who live with it.

FASD can't be cured, but it's not a life sentence. It has made, and continues to make, life a challenge for me. But – and this bit is important – I live a VERY FULL LIFE.

I've been to college and studied make-up artistry. I am a speaker and advocate. I hold down a part-time job. I love sitting in the cinema with a big bucket of popcorn. I've even written this book, and, I don't want to boast, but I've been on the telly too.

If you have FASD, you can lead a full life too.

I know I am lucky; I have the support and love of some amazing people, not least my mum. You'll be hearing from her later. We both wish we could have read about FASD from the perspective of someone living with the condition. We needed to know we were not alone. Some top tips on how to navigate life would have been useful too.

So now I have written my story and included some tips and advice. I hope all of this will help young people, their families, their teachers, and all the people who care for and support them.

Will this book cure FASD? No. Will it help you understand the condition more? Yes. Will you laugh and smile at some of the scrapes I've got myself into? I'm pretty sure you will.

Mostly, I want any of you living with FASD and the people who love you to know that YOU ARE NOT ALONE. There is help and support. Life can be really good.

Right now, understanding of our condition is growing in the wider community. Things are certainly getting better. I hope this book will play its part in making those improvements happen sooner.

Now, about that dinner... A tasty pizza would be nice...

CHAPTER 2

How to Read This Book

This book is not like a novel, where one thing happens, then another thing, then another, until we reach a happy ending.

Don't expect to find that one chapter follows on from where the previous chapter left off.

That's not how my brain works. If you have FASD, that's probably not how yours works either.

When I thought of a new idea or little story to tell you, I wrote it down.

I've tried to organize all the stories about my younger life in the first part of the book, and all the stories about my life now in the second part.

You can start here at the beginning and just read to the end. Or you can dive in anywhere and, I hope, find a chapter or a story that will help you gain a deeper understanding of life with FASD.

If you read a bit and don't feel ready to read more, put the book down, go away. Come back to it when you want to. That's how I read a book.

HOW TO READ THIS BOOK

(I'm going to be honest, putting it down, going away and coming back was how I wrote a lot of this book, too!)

But I do hope you will read all of this book at some point. In learning about my world, I hope you will learn something about yours too.

CHAPTER 3

What Is FASD?

So, what is FASD?

Don't all shout at once!

Yes, it stands for fetal alcohol spectrum disorder. But what is that exactly?

It isn't a disease. There is no medical test for it. You can't analyse a blood sample under a microscope to find out if someone has FASD.

To understand the condition better, it's probably helpful to look at each word individually, going from back to front.

Disorder – Not a disease. A disorder is something which upsets the balance of how your mind or body (or both) function. Imagine a bottle of Coca-Cola. Now imagine shaking that bottle. The Cola starts to fizz and bubble. It's disturbed, it changes. But it's not ill. It doesn't have a disease. That's what a disorder is like. It's not how things should be, but, unlike a disease, a disorder can't be cured with medicine. It needs to be looked after.

Spectrum – A spectrum is something wide-ranging and big. It's like a rainbow. The disorder can't be reduced to one or two symptoms or problems. It involves a whole lot of issues. Remember those 420-plus conditions? I don't have all of them, but I have quite a few. A rainbow of conditions.

Alcohol – Drinks such as beer, wine and vodka contain alcohol, which is a kind of drug. It affects people's behaviour and can make them feel happy. That's why so many people drink it. There are different kinds of alcohol. The type used to make drinks is called ethanol. Ethanol is unfortunately a teratogen.

A teratogen? What is one of those? I'm very glad you asked.
   A teratogen is anything which interferes with the development of a baby in its mother's womb. All teratogens should be avoided during pregnancy. They are like poisons.
   Teratogens zap the cells, the building blocks, of the baby in the womb. They damage parts of the brain and send cells to the wrong places.
   Doctors believe there really is NO SAFE AMOUNT of alcohol you can drink if you are pregnant or trying to get pregnant.

Fetal – This comes from the word 'fetus'. A baby developing in the womb is known as a fetus from around ten weeks into the pregnancy until the child is born. It's the longest stage of pregnancy. Current research suggests that damage can result from alcohol even before ten weeks. Phew, that's a lot of words.

Okay, let's summarize.

LIFE IN THE FASD LANE

> FASD is a disorder (not an illness) that results from the consumption of alcohol while the mother is pregnant. The alcohol acts as a poison on the developing baby. This poisoning can lead to the baby having FASD, and possibly one or more of the 420 physical or neurological (of the brain) co-occurring conditions.

A brain issue

I'll give you an example of a brain issue I live with. I struggle to learn things. When I learn something new, I quickly forget it.

A child might put their hand somewhere hot and cry out in pain. It hurts. But that child has learned not to put their hand there again. Not me, I'll forget that it hurt and do it again. And again. Eventually some things stay in my brain. But it can take a very long time, and a lot of pain, before they do.

Be patient with me.

CHAPTER 4

Neurotypical and Neurodivergent

I want to introduce you to these two very important words.

'Neuro' means anything to do with the brain, like in the word 'neurological' that I mentioned earlier.

'Typical' means something is like other things, but I suspect you knew that.

If you are 'neurotypical' it means your brain works in the ways you would expect. It's standard. It's what people think of as being 'normal'.

Many people are not 'normal' though. Hey, what's normal anyway? Being different is my normal, that's for sure.

'Divergent' means not like other things. So, if you are 'neurodivergent', your brain is different from other people's.

I like the term 'neurodivergent', because it comes without any judgement. It says, 'You are different, and that's okay'. People who live with FASD are neurodivergent.

Describing someone as not 'normal' is really unkind. But being different, well, I'm all up for celebrating that.

Different is good. But being different is also hard and people don't always understand why I do or say the things I do.

23

This can lead to conflict, which adds an extra layer of difficulty in my life.

We live in a neurotypical world. Society, though, has made huge strides in recent years in recognizing neurodiversity.

Neurodiversity? Yes, that's another new word.

'Diverse' means 'many'. There are many kinds of neurodivergence. A diversity of them, you might say.

My key part of my neurodivergence, for example, is my struggle to learn and remember information. Somebody else might struggle to adapt to change. Another person might learn and retain information immediately when it is given to them.

More and more people are coming to understand that not everyone is 'typical'. It's exciting and points to a brighter, happier future for people like me.

I'm trying to channel my neurodivergence into my superpower. A power that allows me to help other young people with FASD.

Now, on with the book.

CHAPTER 5

Growing Up

My early life

The time – ten past ten on a cold February morning.

The place – the maternity unit of the Norfolk and Norwich University Hospital.

Five weeks earlier than expected, a tiny baby, weighing less than a bag of sugar, was delivered by caesarean section. That baby was me, Rossino Jowil Elia-Griffin.

I was so small, the size of a Barbie doll. I could have worn doll's clothes!

I had been struggling to grow inside my mum's womb.

The nurses in the neo-natal intensive care unit were amazing. They had to give me all the nutrients I needed to survive by feeding me via a tube. This went on every 30 minutes for the first few days. Just a tiny bit each feed, until, at last, my stomach was able to hold more.

When tiny me learned to suck properly, Mum was able to help with the feeding too. Because I hadn't gained weight in the womb, I was hungry all the time. I just wanted more food. Not much has changed in that respect!

My mum and dad separated not long after I was born. I did see Dad occasionally, but most of the time I was growing up, it was just me, Mum, my sister and my brother.

Early on I knew I was different. I mean, what three-year-old boy takes a t-shirt and turns it into an off-the-shoulder dress? ME! I kept stealing my sister's make-up to do baby drag. Oh, the fun I had!

At school

It wasn't just my taste for dressing up that set me apart. I didn't behave like other kids at all. At my first school, I really felt like the odd one out. I never stopped talking and was constantly being told to keep quiet.

Luckily, I was surrounded by a loving family. They accepted me for myself. I was different, yes, but it would be a long time before we fully understood how and why.

The teacher called in an educational psychologist. She said I had 'an apparent inability to plan ahead or predict what might happen'.

She had a point.

I was always trying to do the right thing, to please people and make them like me. Mostly I ended up doing the wrong thing. I didn't think things through, and I had no awareness of the consequences of my behaviour.

One of my earliest memories goes back to when I was around four years old, so still quite new to school.

It was clearing up time and we children were tasked with putting away the books, chairs and mats. I chose to tidy the dressing-up corner. That was not on the list of tasks!

On being pointed towards something actually on the list, I threw an almighty tantrum. This ended with me grabbing the teacher's leg and being dragged along the classroom floor clutching her ankle, kicking and screaming. She tried to ignore me, which was quite a feat. I think she thought the 'no attention' tactic would make it stop. It didn't.

When it was over, even I thought, 'Wow! That was an experience! I am definitely not like these other kids.'

New schools, new challenges

Not long after the tantrum, at the age of five, I changed schools. Here too, I had trouble fitting in and focusing. I also started having seizures. The doctors said it was probably epilepsy because of the way I used to shake. I don't remember the attacks, but I remember the pills and the wires they stuck on my head. I had to walk around with those wires on for two days. I hated them, but I loved the attention and the extra sweets. And two days off school, yay!

On top of all my medical issues, it was apparent to my mum, by now, that I was probably gay. She decided I would feel more at home in London than in Norfolk. I think she was right, but I was so sad having to say goodbye to the few friends I had.

So, one year later, we moved to a new area. Another school, more unusual behaviour.

I would sneak out of class and go and eat the food in the breakfast club fridge. Now I had become a thief, although I didn't see it as stealing. I was hungry. There was food in this nearby fridge. I took it. Logical.

It was also around this time that the depression began.

Then came the bullying. I couldn't deal with the other kids, and they couldn't deal with me. Unfortunately, kids can be really unkind to someone who doesn't fit in.

Primary school was hard. The psychologists, the tests, the Education, Health and Care Plans (EHCPs). I was even allocated my own teaching assistant to help me focus. Sorry, Mr AB, you had a really tough job!

As the years passed, and I bounced from one confusing situation to another, my mum was only too aware that the traditional school system was not working for me. She started searching for a school that could cater for my growing needs. I was 11, and it was time for me to transition to secondary school. The local education authority agreed that I needed a specialist placement.

Luck was on my side. We found a specialist institution where I could finally begin to flourish.

The Barbara Speake Stage School is in West London. Ms Speake was still in charge when I started. She was a fabulous lady in glitter, feathers and pearls.

It felt as if I had come home.

CHAPTER 6

Senior School

Eleven-year-old Rossi was off to senior school. It's a big step for any child, but for me there was real potential for this to be very traumatic.

I may have grown physically, but inside I was still little me. Still the Rossi who didn't pick up on *any* social etiquette. I had no idea when to laugh at jokes, or even if something *was* a joke. (I still don't, by the way.)

I was a loner, but a loner who was not afraid to express my eccentric and fabulous style. Think snow boots with cargo trousers, which, by the way, is a look that's very on-trend again as I write this.

At this point I crossed the threshold of the Barbara Speake Stage School: 'Stage' and 'School' in one place! Are you kidding me? I had truly landed the golden ticket! At Barbara Speake I found my personality and really began to flourish.

My EHCP meant that I was allocated a full-time one-to-one teaching assistant, Elle. I called her my 'outside brain'. She had been especially chosen by the principal because she had experience of those on the autism spectrum. Remember, I only had labels of autism, ADHD and dyscalculia at that time.

29

But it was also here that I had some of my hardest times socially. Teenage years are hard for everybody, right? It's the time when people start to find their tribe, the group they belong to.

I didn't have a group and often felt very isolated. Whenever I felt uncomfortable, I would act up to protect myself. In a place dedicated to drama, I was the biggest drama queen of them all. It was my coping mechanism, but it led to my being labelled the BITCH of the class. Hard times.

There I was, doing something I loved – acting, singing and dancing – and yet I still struggled to fit in.

But happily, I did learn a lot and I have my helper, my 'outside brain', to thank for that. Without her, I don't believe I would have managed.

What I learned enabled me to gain a place at the prestigious BRIT School of Performing Arts and Technology. Based in South London, this is the most famous state-funded performing arts school in the UK, and competition to get into it is fierce. Thousands apply but only a few hundred are offered an audition, let alone a place. I was one of them!

My time at the BRIT School has since ended but while I was there in Year 11, I started a course in costume design and make-up. I continued the make-up studies when I moved to the Brushstroke Make Up and Hair Academy at the Netflix studios in Longcross. My ambition now is to teach make-up design to other young disabled people. I want to combine this with my work spreading the word about FASD and supporting others who live with the condition.

Doing make-up makes me happy. You can check out some of the looks I have created on Instagram at @makeupbyrossino

Helping others with FASD makes me happy. So, right now, I am very happy. It's taken me a long time, though.

SENIOR SCHOOL

We never stop learning. Education is lifelong. Sometimes I repeat my mistakes, like I told you before. It can take me a long time to learn something new.

When I look back at my early life, and my time at school, I can definitely say that I have moved on in a positive way. I accept myself more. I am kinder to myself, but I am still trying hard to fit in.

CHAPTER 7

A Little Extra Help: Ups, Downs and Medication

I'll never forget the first time I took my 'focus tablet'. I was 16.

The drug in question is specifically for people who have attention deficit hyperactivity disorder. Having ADHD means that I struggle to concentrate, because my mind is constantly 'on the go'.

I was prescribed this drug to calm my mind and help me to concentrate on what was happening to me NOW.

I took my tablet 30 minutes before school. My first lesson was English and, as I sat in class, a wave of calm energy washed over me. Although I was aware of this unusual feeling, I had a sense of peace so strong that I was able to focus one hundred per cent on my learning.

For the first time in my life, I had no outside distractions.

Afterwards I thought, 'Is this how *everyone else* feels? *All the time?*'

It was a weird, exciting and eye-opening experience for me. That day was one of the most productive days of school ever. I was so geared up, and not in a hyperactive way. It was a joy to be able to learn, helped by my new superpower – focus!

A LITTLE EXTRA HELP: UPS, DOWNS AND MEDICATION

Then I discovered that some superpowers come with a price tag.

Mum picked me up from school and I passed out as soon as I got in the car. I was even more exhausted than usual. I didn't feel very hungry and wouldn't eat much at school, so Mum ensured I ate my supper when I got home, despite my protestations. It is important to have a good healthy diet for my already low energy levels. These were the unwanted side-effects of my medicine.

I had also experienced a major change in the way I viewed my neurodivergent experience. I felt as if I now had a window into how much my life did not resemble that of other 16-year-olds or of my fellow musical theatre students.

I had always wondered when exactly my classmates experienced their lowest lows and their very high highs, like I did. My highs and lows were certainly obvious for all to see, but I never saw anyone else exhibit similar behaviour. I was impressed that they were able to hide their feelings so well.

The 'focus tablet' had given me a glimpse into the neurotypical world and had shown me that their feelings weren't the rollercoaster that mine routinely were.

Over the years, I have experienced so many different energy levels, often in one day! I can think of lots of times when my energy has been seriously low, and I've just had to 'get on with it'.

I'm very proud of myself for getting on with things. Getting out of bed, going to school or work, these can be major achievements. I know many others in the FASD community who experience the same.

I still take my 'focus tablet', but only when I really feel it's necessary.

LIFE IN THE FASD LANE

I know it's not for me to advise whether anyone should take medication, but I do think it's helpful to explore all the options that might help life feel like less of a rollercoaster.

CHAPTER 8

Impulsive? Me?

Impulsivity is when you do things on the spur of the moment. No planning. No thought about how your actions might affect other people.

Let me tell you a story about what happened when I fell in love. Not with a person, but with acting.

As you know, when I was younger, I was always the odd one out. I never felt that I knew as much as the other kids around me. It was as if they had access to secret information that made their lives happier and, frankly, easier than mine.

Our local village hall was home to a weekly kids' drama group. Here at last was a place I could belong. I loved acting and I knew I had talent. I really believed in myself and felt sure I would shine. Indeed, as you know, I went on to attend stage school.

My mum explained to the drama group leader about my autism and ADHD. I hadn't been diagnosed with FASD at that point. This teacher was totally fine about it and told her not to worry, there were lots of boisterous children in the group.

Our upcoming production was *Annie Jr*, in which I was given a small speaking part. Very exciting. I loved every minute of it.

The show was set in the 1930s and I was to sing 'NYC' as part of the ensemble. It's a really fun song with a great tune, one you can really belt out. I was determined to give it my all.

Performance night. The drama group helpers had the unenviable job of either making sure I got onto the stage (lack of focus, again!), or pulling me off stage if I wandered onto it at the wrong time. I did that more than once.

Sometimes I'd go on because I thought the song needed more than the person on stage was giving it, or because it seemed unfair that I wasn't in that bit.

None of this behaviour was planned, by the way. Nor did I understand how disruptive it was if I made an entrance when I wasn't supposed to. No thought processes were involved.

The music began, and this was my cue. I was told to get on stage – NOW! I strode out like a glamorous fashion model and suddenly realized that my mobile phone was in my pocket. Brilliant!

I took out my phone, put it to my ear and began to sing to an imaginary friend down the line.

I sang very loudly.

Annie Jr is set in the 1930s. They didn't have mobile phones back then.

Surely that didn't matter because my impulsive phone singing was adding flavour to the production. Surely my fellow performers were thrilled.

I walked off-stage, buzzing, and was immediately surrounded by a group of horrified mums. Did I not know that I had ruined the song?

IMPULSIVE? ME?

I was baffled.

Why were they telling me off? I mean, if anything they should have congratulated me for having taken this suburban off-off Broadway show to the dizzy heights of a top West End production!

I had added a new and exciting dimension to our little show. Hadn't I?

They didn't think so.

That was when I really learned that not everyone is a fan of fabulous impulsivity.

Of course, when I say learned, that's not exactly true. My brain doesn't easily learn things. A child might put their hand somewhere hot and cry out in pain. It hurts. But that child has learned not to put their hand there again. Not me, I'll forget that it hurt and do it again. And again. Eventually some things stay in my brain. But it can take a very long time, and a lot of pain, before they do.

What? I've said this before? In an earlier chapter? So I did. You see what I mean. I don't learn so easily. I repeat things, especially mistakes.

Me singing into my phone wasn't my first impulsive act.

It certainly won't be my last.

So now you are wondering how I deal with impulsivity.

The trouble with impulsivity is it's...impulsive. You don't know when it will strike, or where. It happens on the spur of the moment.

I find being kind to myself really helps. It's not me, it's my brain. Some of the connections in there don't work as they should. I have to remind myself of that, so I don't get upset at myself for having made a terrible mistake.

What's really helpful is letting people around me know that I have this brain damage and explaining to them that some- times I react to situations without thinking. I find that when I do that, people are patient and understanding.

That's the kind of support we all need!

CHAPTER 9

A Friendship Tale

Maisie and I met at the class welcome party.

We were placed next to each other in the morning session, and when we all returned after a lunch break, Maisie found me and sat right next to me – of her own choice! In my mind, that was it – we were destined to be best friends forever.

This is classic behaviour from a child with FASD. Finding someone you like and deciding you're going to be besties with them almost instantly.

I am a true classic. I make those quick bonds a lot!

But I also indulge in the equally typical behaviour of unintentionally pushing away those close to me.

Maisie and I were walking back to the train station after the first day of class. I think it was me who brought up the subject of friendship. I asked Maisie how long she thought our friendship would last.

That's a pretty intense question to ask someone you've only just met. I did explain that I can sometimes say things without thinking, the kind of things that might hurt or even break a friendship.

39

To lighten the mood, I made a bet with her. No money changed hands, but I bet that our friendship would be over by May, around eight months away. Maisie took the bet and put the date in her phone's diary.

You may be hoping for a happy ending, where we were still friends the following Christmas. I know I was. Sadly, that wasn't the case. By the time May rolled around, our friendship was over.

I really hadn't wanted to offend her, but I would constantly 'put my foot in it'. I would cause hurt by making what I thought was a joke, the more outrageous the better. I do have a habit of making inappropriate jokes when I feel insecure.

Because, outwardly, I look confident, people don't see the insecurity and think I'm just being bitchy.

I lost a friend, but I gained some knowledge about myself. It's rare for someone with FASD to have lots of friends and for those relationships to run smoothly, but I can see the patterns now. To be fair to me, I did try to warn Maisie, but I understand that requiring someone to give me the benefit of the doubt all the time is a lot to ask.

There are certain social norms that we all need to sign up to in order to have lasting relationships. Regularly making jokes at your friend's expense isn't one of them. We need to be kind to our friends, but kind to ourselves too.

Based on my experience of many broken friendships, here's my advice to you:

- Take time with every new friendship. Let it develop. Maybe it won't develop. Not everyone you meet will be your best friend, and that's okay.

A FRIENDSHIP TALE

- Know yourself. Try to be aware of the things you do and say that might hurt other people and your relationships with them. You can try not to do those things, but don't beat yourself up if you do make mistakes.
- Be honest. If you feel a friendship is developing into something that could really be long-lasting, be open about the difficulties you face, and the things you do that might seem odd. A true friend will be supportive of you and your insecurities.
- Be ready to apologize. If you do say or do something that hurts someone, say sorry. A true friend will forgive you.

CHAPTER 10

School Bullies

It won't surprise you to know that, as a socially awkward, very feminine young boy, I was a major target for the school bullies.

Being bullied or excluded by the other kids is something most young people with FASD can relate to. We are different, all of us, but not all in the same way.

Most kids struggle to understand people who are not like them. Bullying is often a response to that. It's a case of 'You're different, I don't get it, you make me feel insecure.' That's when the emotional and physical abuse starts.

Did I stand up for myself?

Absolutely not.

I would just laugh along as the bullies mocked me and called me names. It was as if I was giving them permission to taunt me. I thought that might help me be accepted by everyone.

There was one boy who constantly picked on me, not for being neurodivergent, ironically, but for being gay.

Let's call him Checker.

Checker would point at me, laugh, and say something hurtful. I would shout, 'Stop it, you're a meanie.' Well, that really isn't clever vocabulary for a 13-year-old and did nothing to stop the relentless teasing.

One day, Checker pushed me to breaking point. He said something that just sent me over the edge. I can't even remember what it was now, but I had had enough. Without displaying any emotion, I quietly threw a bottle of water over him. He was drenched.

I thought, 'You're not a very nice guy so this is what you deserve.' I was frustrated that my verbal responses weren't hitting home, so, for once, I had decided that direct action was required. So did he.

He beat me to a pulp in front of everyone. Yes, it was painful, but it achieved the desired effect. He got detention. Unfortunately, because I started the argument, so did I!

Mum wasn't angry with me, thank goodness. In fact, she took me out for a burger at the pub. My brother told me to fight back. 'I can teach you how to throw a punch, Rossi. It's all about defending yourself.' But that wasn't the point. I hadn't wanted to hurt Checker, just get him into trouble.

I feel confident in saying that not one of us with FASD sets out to harm others with our behaviour. But, we also have a right not to be hurt or harmed ourselves. We may be different, but we are people too. We are navigating life, maybe not always successfully, but bullying us if we get it wrong really doesn't help.

I know for myself that being made to feel bad for being different doesn't help me live in this neurotypical world of ours.

Is there a solution? Teaching children about FASD would be a big start, especially if they have a classmate with the condition. Kids bully when they don't understand. Nobody understood me, and I suffered for it.

I'd love for the kids who come after me not to suffer.

CHAPTER 11

A Clinic, a Doll's House and a Pointy Cup

Sitting in the passenger seat on the way to school, I distracted myself from thinking of how the day ahead would go and I thought about the video call I'd had with my friend Gabi the night before. I was around eight or nine years old. I should inform Mum about our decision. The words I used to my mum were, 'I want to be a girl.'

A big announcement, I think you'll agree, and one made with no explanation at all. Poor Mum!

What I had neglected to tell her was that my best friend and I had decided that we wanted to be sisters. Well, that was never going to happen as long as I was a boy. So, it was necessary for me to become a girl.

As you know, I don't make friends easily, so I was determined to be as close as possible to the person I love most. Gabi is still my childhood best friend to this day, as it happens. That shows the strength of our bond. Sister from another Mr.

Mum was very calm, although goodness knows what she was going through. With my words ringing in her ears, she got us an appointment at the famous Tavistock Clinic.

Remember, this was some time before I was diagnosed with FASD and, although we knew something was wrong, we were still exploring exactly what that might be.

Our appointment was with a gender dysphoria therapist. Obviously, I had no idea what that meant; I was just really excited to go into London and explore a place I had never been to before.

According to the National Health Service, gender dysphoria 'describes a sense of unease that a person may have a mismatch between their biological sex and their gender identity'.

In my case, I was born a boy, but felt I really should be a girl. As I told you, deep down I didn't really think that, but I must confess that I enjoyed the attention from the clinic.

As I remember, the Tavistock was a tall grey building. There was a car park at the front and, in the waiting room, a water cooler with the funny-shaped paper cups. Who drinks out of triangles? Could I take them home? They were brilliant.

A triangular cup is a good example of something that is different from what we consider 'normal', but still does the job we expect it to do and does it well. It holds water and we can drink out of it.

It's a bit like me. I have FASD and am neurodivergent. My brain does not behave in a 'normal' way, yet I still study and go to work. You might not expect me to do either of those things. But here I am, doing them well, if I say so myself. Just like the cups.

No sooner had I discovered the joy of these pointy, triangular drinking vessels, than we were guided down a long grey carpeted hallway to the therapist's office. Only then did I start to feel a little nervous.

LIFE IN THE FASD LANE

'We are just going to talk about your feelings about wanting to be a girl, Rossi. It's nothing to be worried about.'

Now, when you tell a little kid not to worry, what do they do? They worry. Big time. At least I did and, being a very dramatic person, I genuinely believed that my 'manhood' was about to be chopped off. In the therapist's room! Right there and then! I could practically see her grabbing a pair of scissors from her desk drawer. 'Come on, Rossi, this won't hurt a bit!'

That's another facet of my FASD. I catastrophize. This means I only see the very worst possible outcome – a catastrophe.

I had to stop this now.

'I don't want to be a girl. I love football and Action Man,' I protested.

Then I shot myself in the foot, so to speak. No sooner had I made that earth-shattering declaration, than I spotted a doll's house in the corner. I was OBSESSED with all things doll related. By dolls, I mean Barbie, NOT Action Man.

I didn't hear another word the therapist was saying. After about ten minutes of what was pure 'blah, blah' to me, I plucked up the courage to ask, 'Can I play with the doll's house now?' And off I ran, into the corner.

We continued to visit the therapist on a monthly basis. I am so grateful to my mum for taking positive action. What she did helped me realize what was really going through my mind.

I didn't want to be a girl. I was struggling with the idea of being a feminine boy who liked singing and dolls. There's nothing wrong with that. It's fine to be who you are. As a gay man, I know that, but it was another layer of difficulty for me as I was growing up.

We still had a long way to go. There were so many other

46

A CLINIC, A DOLL'S HOUSE AND A POINTY CUP

things going on with me, physically and mentally. It would be a few years before I was finally diagnosed with FASD.

I still get excited when I see triangular cups, though. Who invented them, I wonder? They are amazing. There goes my mind, off on a wander again.

CHAPTER 12

A Marble-ous Story

When I was six, I swallowed a marble.

The marble was small, colourful and looked like bubble gum. I put it in my mouth and swallowed it whole. I knew it was glass, but I ate it anyway. Then I carried on with what I was doing before I saw the lovely marble. I even forgot I had swallowed it, until the stomach pains reminded me.

Reluctantly, I confessed all to Mum. She was very concerned, as you would expect, and bundled me into the car for the drive to hospital.

After a short wait in A&E, a doctor called my name and we were led to a cubicle. I climbed on to the bed, pulled up my shirt and the doctor started prodding and poking my belly. I remember thinking, 'This must be what a pregnant woman feels like.' The doctor's hands were big and cold. They were so huge I felt as if I was being examined by a giant.

What happened to the marble? I'm not a hundred per cent sure, but I think it passed through my body in the way you might expect. Please don't ask for any more detail than that!

You'll be pleased to know that I never swallowed a marble

again. I think this incident taught me that even if something looks nice, you really should stop and think before you pick it up and eat it.

As an extra piece of advice, I would say please don't swallow bubble gum, either. It's dangerous. Just like swallowing marbles.

Do you know why I can't remember what happened to the marble? Because none of that ever happened. It's completely untrue. The whole story is made up.

Swallow a marble? Me? Come on.

What six-year-old boy knows anything about pregnancy, let alone what it feels like?

And, yet, in my head, when I wrote this down, I could see it all so clearly. I remembered it as if it was yesterday. It's funny that I couldn't remember the icky bit about what happened to the marble in the end. But the doctor with the big hands? I can see him, and those hands, in my mind's eye right now.

It's called *confabulation*.

This is when a person makes up stories that they believe to be absolutely true, often based on things that have actually happened.

I remember that my mum once accidentally swallowed a penny.

I remember that I made many visits to the hospital for all kinds of different things.

I remember that I owned some marbles.

So, I wove all these things together in my head to make one entirely new story. I didn't even realize that I was making it up. I promise you that when I make up a story, I certainly don't set out to deceive anyone.

That's what confabulationists do. We're not trying to tell lies.

I think I just made up a word, though: 'confabulationists'.

Maybe it isn't a new word, but, in my head, it really is. Or it's the name of a well-known indie band.

Confabulation is yet another way in which my brain is

different. Lots of people tell lies, but they know they are making things up, even if they don't admit it. I wasn't lying, I was telling you what I believed to be true.

Telling a good story is a way to connect with people. I've been a performer, so I know this to be true. Maybe I am using these made-up stories to make myself more interesting and get people to like me. We all love a bit of drama, and what could be more dramatic than a dash to the hospital?

Perhaps I could use this to my advantage. Some people are storytellers by profession. It's their job! I could do that. Maybe I could even write a book. Maybe you'll read it. Oh, wait...

Before we move on, I want you to know that every chapter you read before the marble story is all true. When you turn the page, everything you read from then on is true.

No more confabulation.

I am crossing my heart with one hand (hope NOT to die) as I type this with the other. I promise!

CHAPTER 13

Living With My Brain Now: Dichotomies

What's it like for me right now, living with FASD? Well, life is very much a series of dichotomies.

You may not have come across this word before. It sounds big and fancy, but it just means when two things exist together that really shouldn't. Think of it like dipping your chips in your McFlurry. It's both delicious *and* disgusting. All at the same time. That's a dichotomy.

(I'm not the only one who dips their chips, am I? Surely not.)

I love this word, 'dichotomy', because it describes so many aspects of life with FASD. It's like a Marvel movie inside my head sometimes; a battle between two opposing forces or feelings. But it's not a case of goodies versus baddies.

It's not that one force is better than the other. They are both aspects of me. There's a lot going on, and, honestly, it can be exhausting.

Let me give you some examples.

- **Happy and sad**
    - You ask me if I am a happy person. Yes, I really am. You ask if I am a sad person. I'm very much sad too.

LIVING WITH MY BRAIN NOW: DICHOTOMIES

Wait a minute, how can I be both? I carry these two emotions around with me all the time. Happy one second, sad and depressed the next, then back again to happy. The change from one to the other is so fast, it can make your head spin. Flip, flop. Then flop, flip. This is my life.

- **Hyper and lethargic**
  - Am I an energetic person? Hell, yeah! But then again, no. This is something that I know affects lots of us with FASD.

    I unleash a huge burst of energy. No sooner have I done that, than there's an equally huge slump. I just want to sleep. Sometimes that's followed by another burst of energy, and another slump. Remember I mentioned right at the beginning that I struggle to stay focused? Lack of focus is very much related to my being so 'up' one minute and suddenly 'down' the next. And just to be clear, all this up and down business is nothing to do with being happy or sad. This is about energy levels. When I'm lethargic, in 'down' mode, there can be grumpiness. But I can also be 'down' and actually quite happy.

- **Attention**
  - When I was at primary school and the educational psychologist came to see me, I loved being the centre of attention. Point any light in my direction, darling, and I will bask in its glow. But I also like to hide away by myself.

    You would think that, as a student at the BRIT

53

School, I was totally living my dream, right? Wrong! I loved the build-up to the shows, the beautiful costumes. Dress-up time! But then I decided that I really didn't want people looking at me. Yes, me. The person who couldn't wait to get on stage. I gravitated more towards studying costume design. I could still be creative but behind the scenes. But then I was envious watching the musical theatre performers take their bows to huge applause.

I don't want people looking at me. But I hate it when they don't. What do I really want? Erm, a bit of both?

- **Relationships**
  – Where do I even begin? I often think I'm best friends with someone when I hardly know them.

  I jump ahead, move too quickly.

  I like you so you clearly like me. Or not?

  Will you tell me if you don't? No wait, don't.

  You're my best friend, I met you last week. This week you are ignoring me.

  I'm in love, or am I?

  I want friends, but it's too hard.

  I tell myself to slow down but I don't. The chemicals in my brain are bouncing about, the happy one is taking over.

  Then impulse control! Yes, what impulse control?

  So, you see, I want friends, but I don't.

And breathe...

The relationships/friends thing, it's a big one.

It's so big that I'm going to give it its own chapter. Or maybe I won't? Just joking!

You see, more dichotomies. I want to but I don't.

You may be able to relate to these inner conflicts and possibly have some of your own to add.

CHAPTER 14

Sleep

As I write this, I haven't been sleeping too well. This happens a lot, and when it does, everything else in life starts to fall apart. That's not surprising; I'm really tired.

But I've just had an amazing conversation with my mum that I wanted to share. She says the reason I don't sleep at night is because I don't want the day to end. Or perhaps I don't want tomorrow to come. A little lightbulb lit up in my head because I know she's right.

I huddle in my bed watching hours and hours of television to postpone the moment when I have to go to sleep and then wake up in a whole new day.

It's not that I don't want a new day. But if I'm doing something I love, like watching television, I am shutting off from all the negative emotions, all those dichotomies. I'm watching another world, one in which everything is predictable.

Every night, Mum says, 'Go to sleep'. I know she's right, and that not sleeping is bad for me. It's common for people with FASD to lack the melatonin needed to tell our brain that it is time to stop, switch off and sleep. One of the 420-plus issues we deal with.

SLEEP

Melatonin
Melatonin is a hormone our brains produce when it's dark outside. It's like a little messenger that comes to us by night to tell us it's time to sleep. It makes our eyelids heavy. Unfortunately, the light from our screens – phones, computers, tablets – confuses the messenger, and it thinks it's still daytime. So, it turns around and walks away. No melatonin, no signal that it's bedtime. People lacking in melatonin can take medication to top it up.

I take melatonin medication and it's a great help, but my system gets used to its effects quite quickly and I have to take time off the tablets.

I know it's not easy, but the best thing for us is to create a welcoming environment for natural melatonin. One way to

LIFE IN THE FASD LANE

do this is to switch off all screens *at least 30 minutes* before you go to sleep.

Good advice, I think you'll agree. But easy to follow? Absolutely not!

All the medical advice says we need seven to eight hours, even more if you're under 18. Then you need as many as ten hours a night!

TEN HOURS!

If you have FASD and your brain is constantly whirring away like a machine, creating new thoughts, you REALLY need a good night's sleep.

I don't always get those minimum seven hours. When I do, the new day becomes something welcoming rather than overwhelming. It takes determination and practice, but it's possible.

I am working on finding a calming routine that really does the business. Yes, screens off, I know.

I have to keep reminding myself of the joy of a new day full of energy. That helps me to switch off (literally!) and calm down.

Full-night's-sleep Rossi? He's a powerhouse. You'd be amazed by what he can do.

CHAPTER 15

Everybody Needs a Safe Space

What is a safe space?

It's somewhere you can shut out all the social stress and be yourself.

It's a place to recharge your batteries.

A place you can do what you want at your own pace.

A place where you can return to a state of calm.

I think we can agree that everybody needs a safe space, but it's even more important if you have FASD.

My safe space is my bedroom at home in Surrey.

I find familiarity comforting. Our house is the place I know best. It's where I spent most of my childhood. It's where my mum, my greatest supporter, lives too. Within the house, my bedroom is the place that's most familiar.

In my room are my bed and my television. I can huddle under the duvet with my headphones on and watch a three-hour Marvel film, uninterrupted.

Back when I was small and we were living in Norwich, my safe space was my sister's bedroom. I can still recall the Avril Lavigne CDs, the Britney perfume, the Juicy Couture bedding.

Her room was everything I wanted in a room of my own. It was full of fabulous clothes, which I regularly borrowed, even though I was quite a bit smaller than she was!

Now I do have my own room, full of things I love. I retreat there often. Just me, my brain and my favourite superheroes. I think of this film-watching as my Safety Habit; the habit, or routine, which helps to calm my brain down. And it's best done in my Safe Space. The routine is very comforting. I can watch the same film over and over again and be as involved in it as the first time I saw it. It's not unusual for me to shout at an actor, 'Don't open that door! Don't go in there!' I'll be deep into something (my film in this case), but without actively doing anything – except the occasional shouting! I am totally swept away by the film, but without having to do anything myself.

The fantasy world becomes my world for a while.

The result – zero stress.

Of course, my Safety Habit has changed with time. It used to be much more active and involve a lot of drawing. Or slapping on some make-up and doing drag. Because I do make-up all week now, I don't really want to do it to calm down. It takes a lot of energy to do it well. So, you'll find me watching television or sometimes listening to music. (Actually, you won't *find* me, because I'll be doing this alone, in my safe space!)

I'm happy to be passive and let the nice people who make Marvel films do all the work.

As we grow up, habits – and needs – change. That's what I have found, anyway.

Don't fight it, I say.

What kept you safe and happy last year, might not do the same for you now. Find your new safety habit and go with it for as long as it helps you.

EVERYBODY NEEDS A SAFE SPACE

We change, we grow up, and our habits can change too. Music has been a constant for me, although what I listen to in order to calm my brain has changed. Before it was all Ariana Grande. Now I get totally lost in Griff, Lana del Rey and Abba. I mean, who doesn't like a bit of Abba!

So, what is your Safe Space?

Do you have a Safety Habit?

It's good to have a place to retreat to, but yours will be different from mine. Remember, too, that the place can change. It all depends on where life takes you. Wherever you find yourself, I would really encourage you to create your own safe space.

If we are on holiday, my first thought is often, 'Where can I create a Safe Space for myself here?' It's not always easy if we are in a hotel, but it's worth a try. It helps both me and my mum.

I also indulge in my Safety Habit wherever and whenever I need to calm my brain down.

Right, I am off to my bedroom. I'll be back with you in a while!

CHAPTER 16

A Literal Basket Case

I take things literally.

If you tell me you're drowning, I might call 999 to get the Coastguard to rescue you. It won't occur to me that by 'drowning' you mean you are 'busy'.

Perhaps you are 'up to your eyeballs' in work. Now I picture you surrounded by piles and piles of paperwork, literally up to the height of your eyes.

Please, never play a practical joke on me. I won't understand it, nobody will laugh, and it might all end in tears.

I also forget things. If you give me too much information, I will only remember a small portion of it.

Taking things literally and forgetting stuff – sometimes these two combine to cause maximum confusion.

A while back, my mum gave me a list of chores to do. This list was verbal, not written. She just told me what needed to be done. Mum had forgotten that if you give me multiple things to do, the chances are most of them won't get done. That's not me being lazy, I just can't help it. Most of what you have said will have gone in one ear and out of the other, as if it's drained out of my brain.

A LITERAL BASKET CASE

- Clean your room.

  - Hoover the floor.

    - Bring me your washing basket.

A simple enough list, but by the time I had reached the top of our stairs the cleaning and the hoovering were long forgotten. The washing basket, on the other hand, well, I was supremely confident about that particular task. I tipped all my dirty clothes onto the floor and ran down the stairs. Mum was waiting to load the washing machine when I presented her with the empty basket. She was baffled.

'You said to get the laundry basket, here you go.'

Now I had thought it was a bit odd that she would ask just for an empty basket, but, in my mind, I was following her instructions. What she really wanted was its contents, so she could wash my clothes. Said contents were lying in a heap on my bedroom floor.

They did get washed eventually – I do like my clothes to look their best – but not until Mum had explained, with total clarity, what she wanted from me.

My advice: Lots of people with FASD take what is said literally. Lots of people with FASD struggle with short-term memory.

If you have FASD:

- Never be afraid to ask if you have understood the question or instruction properly. Tell the person what you think they have just asked you to do, to check that it's correct.

If you don't have FASD:

- Be patient with us!
- Be clear in your instructions. Check that we have un-

A LITERAL BASKET CASE

derstood fully. It might feel patronizing to ask us to tell you what you have just told us, but it does help to avoid a lot of misunderstandings.

- Don't give us too many instructions or pieces of information at once. Think about the one thing that's most important and just give us that for now. Give us time to absorb the information, or do the required task, before presenting us with something new.

CHAPTER 17

The Best Form of Defence?

When I was very young, I wanted to fit in with everyone else, but I didn't know how to. The other kids knew I was different, so they bullied me.

At the age of eight, and very impressionable, I learned what I thought was an important lesson – attack is the best form of defence.

Which first-class educator was responsible for this amazing revelation? The 2004 film, *Mean Girls*.

To this day, my mum hates that film and that the message I took from it was, 'If they're mean to you, be mean right back.' Of course, I know now that this isn't right. But to eight-year-old me, this film had it all. It was girly, sassy and full of pink. In my formative fashionista years, it was highly appealing.

In the story, Regina, the mean girl, is horrible to people she thinks are different or not good enough. The nice girl, Cady, is truly nice and doesn't want to be mean to anybody. She becomes friendly with the mean girl. But this doesn't keep her safe from all the meanness. Cady decides to fight fire with fire. She gives back the sass she has been subjected to and is mean to the mean girls, all the while dressed in fabulous pink.

THE BEST FORM OF DEFENCE?

It was a lightbulb moment for me. I, too, could be sassy and pink and give right back to my mean girls what they were giving me. I used to recite actual biting lines from the film.

Did it work? Err, sort of. I did find myself in trouble more often. My bullies would run to the teacher, crying and saying I had been mean to them. The teacher would tell them to stay away from me. Well, that was a win for a start! It cut the bullying right down, as they didn't come near me.

So, I learned that if I wanted to be left alone, or not made to feel stupid, my best tactic was to make a verbal attack.

Later, at college, I was surrounded by other creative arts students. I was up against equally sassy divas. I continued my primary school playground *Mean Girls* behaviour. But it didn't have the same effect. My sassy quotes from the film now came across as childish.

My response to bullying had to change, but I had no idea how. I just became meaner and bitchier. I also became more isolated.

I wish it had been different, but having FASD means that, even though I was the same age as the other kids, I wasn't developing socially at the same pace as them. I didn't understand this, and it made me angry that I was always getting things wrong. I was angry with my fellow students, with my teachers, with my mum, and with life in general. Attack remained my best form of defence.

Of course, at the root of much of this is a lack of self-confidence. Even now, I still perceive innocent questions as an attack on me. After a lifetime of constantly being 'in the wrong', I hope you can understand that. For example, Mum might ask me if I have put my clean clothes away. My brain immediately goes into defence mode and I start shouting, attacking her for

LIFE IN THE FASD LANE

doubting me. I just want her to stop going on at me, and this is the quickest way my brain knows to make that happen.

But it was just a question.

That I am even able to write all of this shows that I have grown in terms of understanding my own behaviour. It doesn't mean I always do the right thing. I still see most questions as designed to trick me, especially if I am tired.

I know that constantly attacking people is getting me nowhere, but making a more permanent change to my reactions is taking me lots of time.

Not for the first time in my story, I am asking for your patience.

Rossi's tips

- To help avoid the attacks, the meanness, and to support me, or someone else with FASD, the most important thing is *clarity*.
- Be clear when speaking to us – signpost that you are not attacking us. This helps in understanding that we don't need to go on the defensive.
- An opening sentence like this might help: 'I have something to tell you that isn't an attack on you, it's some helpful advice.'
- I, and others like me, need to learn that critiques aren't always negative, that advice is given to help make things better.
- If I (or someone else you know) reacts badly to this, ask again, 'How do you feel? Why is that? What can I do to make you feel better?'

THE BEST FORM OF DEFENCE?

Eventually, your care and support will reinforce the message that meanness gets you nowhere.

To be honest, that's the message of *Mean Girls* too. I just chose to look past that and focus on the pink sassiness. It wasn't my best move.

CHAPTER 18

Focus, Focus

Concentration brain overload.

Does your brain have a ranking system for doing things? Does it decide what things are important to get done based on its own, maybe not totally logical, categories?

Mine does.

And the ranking, the categories, the priorities, can all change depending on my mood. My mood is affected by a ton of different factors:

- How tired I am.
- What else I've been doing that day.
- What else I am asked to do.
- Hunger.

Take this book, for example. I know I have to write it. The publisher has given me a deadline and I need to crack on. So writing is obviously my number one priority right now. Right? Wrong.

Or maybe it's right sometimes.

FOCUS, FOCUS

Today I am writing. My brain has told me that writing is my number one priority today. It's entirely possible I may just write three whole chapters in the next hour. How's that for being productive?

Other days I am thinking to myself, 'Writing? No, that's not important at all.' Then I am filing all thoughts of writing in the furthest reaches of my brain.

But that back part of the brain can get full, and the important things, like writing a book, get pushed forward and cause me huge stress.

If you hide something, it doesn't go away. If you neglect doing something, it will still need to be done.

I'll be honest and tell you that I have been doing this a lot recently, neglecting things. I have pushed aside coursework and book writing and prioritized sleeping and television watching. This is me taking a mental break from the daily stress of college life and trying to escape my responsibilities. The concentration filing cabinet drawer in my brain is full up and getting messy.

Sleep is good, of course, but you can have too much of a good thing.

Try asking me, or anyone with FASD, why we lie in bed all day. We'll tell you, 'I'm tired!' You will wonder how that can possibly be when we've been doing absolutely nothing except lying in bed.

Life is tiring. Just being alive and even something as simple as breathing can overwhelm me. When external stress gets too much and my filing cabinet brain is full up, I shut down, go to bed and don't talk to anyone. I'm not being lazy. I literally have no energy left to concentrate. That's what FASD can do to me – it robs me of all energy and drive.

LIFE IN THE FASD LANE

Then I need space and time to recharge the batteries.

Well, look at that. I just wrote a whole chapter. I hope it was helpful and insightful. Writing it was certainly helpful for me. I feel surprisingly energized.

Maybe I'll write another chapter, right now!

(UPDATE: I didn't. It was ages before I wrote another chapter!)

CHAPTER 19

OCD, TAF: Scary Thoughts, an Elephant and Pizza

My mum is an imposter.

I have been kidnapped, bundled into a car and driven away from my hometown in Sicily. Now I am living in Surrey with my sister, my brother and this imposter lady. She is not my real mum.

I know my sister and brother are my real sister and brother. I know that the imposter mum is *their* real mum. But she is not *my* real mum. I am in a panic.

I go to look at my imposter mum to make sure I am right. She is relaxing in front of the television. She turns and smiles at me. She sees I am distressed and sits up. 'What's the matter? Are you okay? What's happened?'

I turn and flee. The kidnapper lady is nice, and I feel bad that I am thinking she is a bad person. But I can't get the thought that she is not my real mum out of my head!

She calls up to my sister, 'Jodie, can you check on Rossi? Has something happened?'

All this took place a long time ago, but it's so clear in my mind. I can still recall the fear.

73

Jodie sat with me, I buried my head in her lap and she reassured me that the lady was my mum too, not just hers and my brother's. She explained it was not logically possible for it to be otherwise. She assured me that she wouldn't make things up and that it was probably my OCD TAF making my head do silly things.

Let me explain both OCD and TAF.

Obsessive compulsive disorder (OCD) is when you are fixated on an unwanted thought that won't go away, or you feel that you have to repeat a certain behaviour over and over to help you relieve your feelings of anxiety. We often think of people who are afraid of germs and keep washing their hands again and again. That's certainly one manifestation of OCD, but there are others.

Thought-action fusion (TAF) is something slightly different, but related. This is where a person has intrusive thoughts and believes that merely thinking about something can actually make it happen. It's possible I had seen something on television which made me believe I had been kidnapped. Or perhaps I had been playing with my Barbie dolls and the thought came into my head. That's less likely, as Barbie time was happy time. I should point out that I was nine years old when all this happened (just in case you are imagining a 22-year-old me playing Barbie and Ken – although Barbies still make me smile!).

These thoughts can trigger OCD symptoms, so you can see how linked they are.

The imposter lady episode, as we have come to know it, was very scary. At the same time as 'thinking' it was real, I knew it was not. At the same time as wanting to get away from that lady, I wanted her to make me feel better. I understood that she

OCD, TAF: SCARY THOUGHTS, AN ELEPHANT AND PIZZA

was my real mum, but only because Jodie had explained how it could not be otherwise. How terrifying is that?

Jodie asked if I had watched the news. I'm not supposed to watch the news because it has some scary stuff on it, and it can affect me. 'No, no honestly I haven't!' Well, maybe I had. Maybe I had seen a news item about an imposter lady that had triggered the TAF.

Things grew less intense as Jodie reminded me of how my brain goes off on tangents and that the intensity of my feelings meant I couldn't separate the real from the imagined. I needed her calm voice to settle my intrusive thoughts. Her mum was my mum – our real mum.

As I let our mum hug me, I was more worried that she might be sad. She reassured me that she understood, she wasn't sad and she said that I should go and sit with Jodie until I felt better. I stayed with Jodie until the fear passed.

Sometimes it can take a few days, even weeks for those horrible experiences to fully heal. It is as if they leave a scar in my mind. But I know it is TAF.

I had a lovely psychologist at the child and adolescent mental health services as I was growing up. Let me share with you an interesting exercise we did.

Ready?

Step one: Okay, now, please, whatever you do, DO NOT think about pizza.

What are you thinking about?

It's pizza, isn't it? Of course it is.

Step two: Now, I want you NOT to think about pizza.

LIFE IN THE FASD LANE

Still thinking about pizza? Okay.

Instead, DO NOT think about a big grey elephant sitting in the corner wearing a pink tutu eating the pizza.

I bet you can see that elephant very clearly in your mind's eye.

Feel free to change the colour of the tutu!

You see how we can think things even when we don't want to. And *all* of this is okay. We all behave like this. But most people will move on from pizzas and elephants quickly enough.

OCD is the process of letting that thought continue, getting stuck in it, going over it in your head so many times. This is called *perseveration*.

Yes, it's another new (and long, sorry) word for you. You may never have heard it before, because, unless you have TAF or OCD, you probably don't do any perseverating.

The psychologist gave me tools to unstick my thoughts. She helped me move from my intrusive thoughts by creating a character in my mind that I was able to visualize. This helped me so much. Now, if I feel TAF bubbling up, I think, 'Oh, here comes Vangy.'

Vangy is the most stunning looking drag queen. Huge lips and massive eyebrows. Super gorgeous! Six foot tall and Valley hot pink heels to die for, darling! She is a funny, fabulous and flawless diva! She is a very amusing character and this 'visual' moves me away from the perseverating scary thoughts.

Vangy is not real, as I made her up. But she is a very funny character and visualizing her helps me to shift from thought A to thought B quite quickly.

If you struggle with TAF, or OCD, talk to a therapist or

your parents or carers, so that you can get some tactics to help you through. Everyone is different, so what works for me may not work for you. You might need a different 'helper' from my Vangy. But you can enjoy finding your own character.

Many years on, Mum and I can talk about the imposter lady episode. As much as it was horrid at the time, it was the beginning of me finding ways to help myself in all sorts of situations.

Now, Vangy, how about we don our tutus, go sit with Nelly and grab some of that pizza? We've earned it.

CHAPTER 20

Distracted

So, you might think I've already told you about my distracted mind in the chapter about focus, right? Wrong. You see, to keep focus on something is making sure I do something correctly, and on time. Something important.

To be distracted is when something takes me off track, I'm not tired, my filing cabinet brain is not yet full, so there is enough space to 'think' about something else, other than the task at hand. For example, today, Mum asked me to group my washing into piles of whites, socks and underwear, and dark colours. I organized my jewellery collection instead. A piece of jewellery was on the floor next to my laundry basket and once I picked up this shiny, glittery thing all thoughts of washing went from my head.

Then I heard Mum's frustrated yells echoing up the stairs asking if my other maid had sorted out my washing yet and if not, I needed to sack them. Very witty, my mum.

Cleaning my room in general is always an occasion for much distraction. So many things to organize and put in places other than the floor. Don't get me wrong, I really love it when my room is tidy and clean, in order and with fresh sheets on my bed. It is a really happy place for me.

Getting it to that point, and keeping it there, is a skill I have yet to achieve. I'll be tasked with hoovering and suddenly I'm deep-cleaning my windowsill. Scrubbing away with a washcloth and surface cleaner because my new make-up brush, which I managed to save from the jaws of certain death in the hoover, would look fabulous on display in a jar on said windowsill.

My brain gets fixated on certain things. A lot of people with FASD also have OCD or something similar. I am one of them. This causes me to hyper-fixate on one specific thing, which, most of the time, is completely unrelated to the job I've been given. I explained my OCD in another chapter. Have you read it yet? Ah, okay, I won't mention it again.

If you give me multiple things to do, it's as if a swarm of bees have flown into my head. All I hear is non-stop buzzing. Rather than try and separate the bees and divide the tasks into a kind of to-do list, I just home in on one task, and focus on that, even if it wasn't on the list in the first place.

I remember a few years ago I had to go and stay at my dad's house in Norfolk as my mum needed a break. We had spent weeks arguing, the state of my room being one of the main issues. It was a mess. Mum had tried lots of different strategies to get me to organize things.

We had got rid of unnecessary clothes. We had emptied boxes of bits of paper that should have gone in a bin the last time I attempted to tidy my room. Still, when I hoovered the floor, all kinds of things ended up inside the hoover until it stopped working! Assuming I hoovered the floor at all.

I have to be on my best behaviour at Dad's place all the time.

LIFE IN THE FASD LANE

I must remember to pick up my plate and put it in the dishwasher. I must pick up my mess and not leave it on the floor.

By day three, I was desperate to go home. I called Mum, promising I would never ever make a mess again and that I had learned my lesson. She told me I didn't have to promise her anything, she was just having a rest. I had no choice but to wait this hell out.

One week later, I returned home. It felt like longer, I must say.

But wait, this wasn't my bedroom! I saw new wallpaper, a carpet with no mascara stains and lovely new bedding. All in green, my favourite colour. There were new boxes on Ikea shelves, all neat and tidy and labelled. New drawers, an amazing hanging rail. The mess was all gone. It was glamour and glitz; it was perfect!

I was sent to my dad's so Mum could do all of this. I was so happy I could have cried. I promised to keep it all tidy.

Did I keep my promise? What do you think?

Fast forward to today and I am cleaning. Oh, yes. I am cleaning down the windowsill with something in a spray bottle. That's good. But it isn't what I was asked to do. I got distracted and have neglected to pile the clothes into whites and darks and pants. I walked over the shoes and papers on the floor and didn't know where to start. So, I am drawn to the windowsill.

I'm thinking of sending myself to my dad's house for a week! Distraction is a curse, but it does have its good side. It really does stop the overwhelming confusion I feel when I must be organized. The problem is when it's the wrong thing. Who needs a shiny windowsill, when you've run out of clean clothes?

At least now I understand that my brain is still learning.

One day, I will be able to keep on track and avoid distraction much better. If not, I might just have to earn lots of money to pay the other maid.

For now, I embrace my distracted brain, my spotless windowsill and my brilliant and tidy assortment of jewels and make-up brushes!

Rossi's tips

By all means, give me something to do. But, please, just one thing at a time. Ask me to repeat your instruction, so you know I have understood. Check in with me. Am I doing what was asked of me? If not, do I need some more help, perhaps further instructions? I don't mind if you do this, and I don't feel patronized. It's always better to check. As someone who often gets things wrong, there's a lot of joy for me in a job well done. I just need a bit of help to do the right job.

Feel free to borrow this tip for yourself and share it with anyone who gives you stuff to do. (There's always someone, right?)

Maybe we should make some badges saying, *Just one thing at a time, please!*

That sounds fun. I could do that now.

Oops, there I go again, getting distracted.

CHAPTER 21

Independence

If you were to meet me right now, you would think, 'Well, he comes across as a very capable young man.' You would be right. I am capable of many things.

I can talk the talk. I can hold a good, flowing conversation. I can even add in the odd comical vibe. I look good (thank you), and I can promote myself well. Think of me as a fairly average person but with buckets of extra personality.

Behind all of that, though, I am a young adult who has real difficulties with social interaction. I also struggle to look after myself and, very specifically, to spend money responsibly. I am not yet able to be left unsupervised in my own home. As I write this chapter, I am staying with a family friend in Manchester. Mum is away, and me being here means she doesn't have to worry about my irresponsible and impulsive behaviours.

I could be upset with Mum for arranging for me to stay here, but I see it as a positive. It is giving me the chance to accept that it takes me a bit longer to get to the starting line than the other runners, if I can use a sporting metaphor. They're all lined up and ready to go, and I am still deciding what colour tracksuit would best match my trainers.

INDEPENDENCE

I AM capable and I CAN be trusted, but everything takes time, and I might just end up making a rash, impulsive choice in the meantime.

I am going to blow my own trumpet here and say I am a great make-up artist. But you knew that, right? Selling myself in order to get jobs doing make-up is also something that comes fairly easily to me. Within the make-up world, I feel confident. It's a world that needs my talent, and I am happy to say so.

So, I get the make-up job, hurrah! Now comes the administration: planning the travel, buying the tickets, timetables that must be stuck to, trains that must be caught!

Not forgetting also to check my calendar to make sure I am free on the agreed date in the first place. Yes, it's happened. More than once, I have let a trail of people down because I didn't remember to check the calendar.

Mum and I are currently trialling a new calendar that can be shared, so everyone can see if I am available or not. (Rolls eyes and sighs.)

Seriously, I can't handle all this stuff independently. So, with the help of my personal assistant (PA)/Mum, who takes on the business side, the tricky parts, I can focus on the job at hand and not worry about all the extra stuff that goes with it.

In time, I will be able to do all these things for myself, I am sure. It's just taking me longer to get to that point than most other people.

My independence is growing slowly, like a fabulous wisteria plant. It looks marvellous, but, oh my, doesn't it take a long time to flower! A wisteria also loses its blossom over the winter and must grow again next spring. Well, that I can relate to. If I don't do something for a while, I have to learn how to do it again, but each time I do it, I remember more than the last time.

You're probably wondering if this makes me impatient. Well, yes it does, and that can be a big problem. It is frustrating because I know what needs to be done. For example, a train needs to be booked to get me to, say, Coventry, by 10am. But Mum stops me from agreeing to the job in Coventry until the calendar is checked. And all I want to say is, 'Yes, I'll do it' and run straight to the station with my make-up kit.

She says no, we need to check everything first. So, I fight back. Not in an aggressive way, more in a defiant 'I'm a Survivor' by Destiny's Child kind of way. I guess it's a question of pride. I forget sometimes that Mum is there to help me on my journey to independence.

I will probably always need a PA of some kind, and I should be grateful for that. This person (currently my mum) can take on the tasks that would send me down the wrong path, a path that can lead to the edge of a cliff.

This leaves me to focus on the 'I can' things, like my make-up artistry.

I've already been growing slowly in independence for 22 years. This sweet wisteria plant will keep on growing and in a few more years will blossom into a beautiful, strong, self-confident Rossi who might need a little extra help once in a while. And that will be perfectly fine.

CHAPTER 22

Brain Domains

Have you ever seen a picture of a human brain? It's all grey and bumpy on the outside. Not pleasant to look at, to be honest. But under all those humps and bumps, it's an amazing machine, working 24/7, even when we are asleep.

For the computer nerds among you, it's like a server sending out and receiving messages from all our body's functions.

Unfortunately for me, my brain isn't always working as well as it should. That's what makes me neurodivergent. If you remember, 'neuro' means brain, and 'divergent' means different. I am 'brain different', if you will.

Lots of studies have been done to identify the brain domains affected by FASD.

Wait, what's a brain domain?

A domain is really an area. Our brains, under the humps and bumps, are made of lots of different areas.

Think of the brain like a house, and the areas are the different rooms in that house. Now think about your house, and the various rooms in it. Let's take the bathroom as a good example. In it, I'd expect to find a bath/shower, basin and loo.

LIFE IN THE FASD LANE

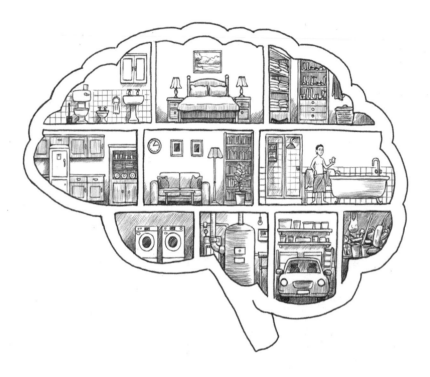

But what if there's no running water in the bathroom? There I am, wrapped in a towel, rubber duck in hand, ready for my bath, but I can't have one.

Is that bathroom really a bathroom? Without water, it doesn't function as one. It's still there but it's not doing its job effectively.

Don't even get me started on the kitchen where the cooker doesn't work, or the living room with no television!

It's the same with my brain. All the rooms are there, but sometimes it's a struggle for me, as they don't always function as effectively as I need them to.

There are ten brain domains – ten 'rooms' – that have been identified as being affected by FASD:

BRAIN DOMAINS

1. **Academic skills**

   (*Maths, abstract concepts like time/money, comprehension, organization/IQ*)

   This means doing well at school. Did I do well? In some subjects, yes. Let's think of this first room as having a number of small cupboards, which represent our school subjects. In the more creative cupboards, I did very well – the ones marked art, dance and English. The more purely academic subjects like maths and science were more of a struggle. To be honest, all of school was a struggle. As I've told you, I find the classroom a difficult place to be. But I do have natural ability in some areas.

2. **Attention**

   (*Overstimulation, being impulsive, over-active, lack of attention*)

   Sorry, what did you say? As I said at the beginning of this book, focusing on one task at a time is a real challenge.

3. **Cognition**

   (*Reasoning and thinking, understanding complex ideas, learning/memory*)

   A slightly fancy word, this, for problem-solving and understanding difficult ideas. I'm not great at problem-solving or thinking ahead. I also struggle to understand the consequences of my actions.

4. **Language and communication**

   (*Expressive and receptive language, difficulty following instruction, speaking well but not understanding full meaning*)

I told you I have natural ability in some areas. Oh, yes. Words, words, words. I love them. I love speaking. I love writing, when I can focus for long enough to do it. But when you speak to me, or give me instructions, unless your words are clear, simple and without any frills, I may not take everything in. Now this definitely has consequences!

5. **Memory**
   (*Long-/short-term memory, recall of sequencing, tendency to fill in blanks and repeat mistakes*)
   A lot of information comes my way every day. I struggle to remember it all. Then when I repeat some of that information to you, I might just fill in my memory gaps with something I have completely made up. I am not deliberately lying, I'm just making sure I tell you a complete story, even if it's not the right one.

6. **Brain structure/neurophysiology**
   (*Head circumference size may be small, neurological diagnoses or disorders*)
   When we are born, we get our head measured to check for things that might be different from the average. If the 'circumference' is smaller than is expected, this could mean that the brain is also smaller. Imagine that your bathroom functions perfectly well but is a little too small to fit everything in and you have to stand on the loo to take a shower! That makes things a little tricky, right? Size isn't everything, but it sure makes a difference!

BRAIN DOMAINS

7. **Executive functioning**
    (*Planning, sequencing, problem-solving, organization, emotional control, transitioning*)
    This is related to 'Cognition' (number 3) and is really being able to deal with everyday challenges. I'm ticking lots of boxes here. Not being the best at executive functioning for me means:

    a. Impulsive behaviour.
    b. Repeating mistakes.
    c. Difficulty understanding abstract ideas.
    d. Difficulty understanding cause and effect.

    Any of these ring a bell with you? I'm devoting a whole chapter to abstract ideas and abstract thinking later. It's so important and deserves more space.

8. **Adaptive behaviour**
    (*Life skills, everyday tasks, self-care, social vulnerability*)
    This is about social skills and knowing how to behave around other people in a way that's right for the situation. Another tick list for me, I think:

    a. Lack of understanding of personal boundaries. (Very much a Rossi thing.)
    b. Easily taken advantage of. (Oh, yes!)
    c. Socially and emotionally immature. (Another oh yes from me!)
    d. Struggling with money. (I am SOOO bad at budgeting, as my mum will tell you.)

9. **Sensory and motor skills**

   (*Fine and gross motor skills, dexterity, sensory issues with light, noise, smell*)

   Nothing to do with cars. This is about physical co-ordination and reflexes. Some people end up with spidery writing because they are unable to hold their pencil properly. Yep, that's me. Trouble learning to ride a bike. Happily, not me. We are all different.

   Oh, I also have a tremor (shaking) in my right hand – another of the 420-plus co-occurring conditions. Excuse me for not telling you earlier – it's my memory and I sometimes only remember issues when they crop up.

   Smells and lights in shops can often trigger sensory overload for me, so I now know which shops to avoid.

10. **Mood**

    (*Anxiety and mood, and managing them*)

    This is a busy room in the house that is my brain. My mood can be all over the place. Happy one minute, sad the next. Low energy, then hyper. There's something called 'affect regulation', which is a person's ability to control their emotions, so they are appropriate to the situation. Imagine being massively furious and crying because someone left the cap off the toothpaste! All of this relates to point 8 about adaptive behaviour.

Ten rooms. Ten domains. Ten things that neurotypical people might find a doddle. Not for me. If you look back at some of the stories from life that I've already told you, you can match some of the stories with these domains.

BRAIN DOMAINS

Genuinely, I am not asking for your sympathy. No 'awws', please. The very best thing you can do is to understand these differences of mine and adjust your behaviour and your expectations of me. So many times, I've become super anxious, because I'm sure I've done something terribly wrong. I've even been told off for bad or disruptive behaviour. But I really didn't mean whatever it was I did in a bad way. I didn't think my actions through (see number 3). I wasn't able to adapt my behaviours and emotions to the situation (see numbers 8 and 10).

I really do find it hard to see things from other people's perspective. I know it's a lot to ask for you to see things from mine. But if you can, it will benefit both of us and help me to be the best person I can be.

CHAPTER 23

Adulting With a Puppy Brain

Having a dog will be brilliant, people said.

It will help your growing independence and self-awareness, they said. It will bring stability and structure to your life.

Well, that all sounded too amazing to turn down.

So, I got a dog.

I *could* tell you that having a puppy was easy. But that would be a lie, and not the unintentional kind of lie that people with FASD often tell. You know, the 'confabulation' lie that we truly believe in, even though it's clearly not true.

Having a puppy was as hard as hell. I wondered if this was what it was like to have a new baby. If so, hats off to all new mums. I genuinely had no idea that having a dog in my life would be such a crazy adventure.

She was always there, always following, always biting and whining when I put her in her crate at bedtime. We called her the 'Velcro dog', because she was always by my side. Sounds cute and adorable, doesn't it? It was at times, but mostly I was finding all the attention and neediness very hard to adjust to. Having FASD means I like routine. I guess I still had a routine, but it was wildly different from the one I had before she arrived.

Even slight changes in my routine can lead to disaster later in the day, week or month. It's a butterfly effect where even a minor mishap can lead to a major breakdown.

That said, I was kind of getting used to the 7am wake up times and the early morning walks. Yes, you read that correctly – 7am! Every day! That was a big change for me. I'm used to my own pace of life and having no responsibility for anything. Suddenly I had charge of a small, but growing, living being. Is this what independence feels like?

I learned that I couldn't be selfish about my actions. In the morning, I heard the alarm and was *straight* up. Before I'd even registered that I was awake, I was already downstairs opening her crate and taking her outside to go to the loo. Sleepwalking almost, but aware that she was my dog and I had to take care of her needs.

Between 8am and 10am, I had to play with her ALL the time! We tried to take her out between 11am and 2pm, then bring her home again for lunch. Then more play. Not forgetting her regular toilet breaks. Around 5pm, she had a nap. This gave me some much-needed rest time.

I really wanted her training to begin, so, I could take her for walks and not be afraid of her eating a slug or cigarette butt!

But it was oh so exhausting. As Mum always says, 'It's not all Sky Movies!' I found myself getting stressed, which made me both angry and lethargic. Before the arrival of the puppy, lethargy would send me off hiding in my room for days, only coming down for food. I would lie down and let my brain rest. Now I couldn't do that. I had a puppy to take care of. I couldn't leave her alone. Had that changed me? Well, yes. Now, I was lethargic, but with a dog.

I was also overstimulated, but with a dog.

I was sure it would all settle down in time, and that I would not regret getting a dog.

All it would take was a little patience.

* * *

I don't have a puppy any more.

I'm both sad and relieved at the same time.

I originally got a puppy in the hope that it would teach me how to be independent and to be more responsible. While it definitely taught me responsibility, the stress of having a living thing to look after day in and day out was just too much.

I was always getting up early, always responsible for watching her all day. It was hard. For some people I know with FASD, a dog is a brilliant companion. For me, and the way *my* FASD works, it just wasn't right.

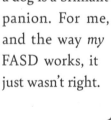
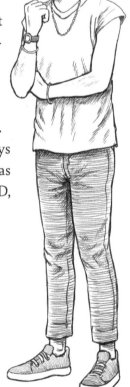

I wasn't able to provide her with the level of affection, care and attention that she deserved and needed.

With it just being myself and my mum, our household was too small for an energetic dog. It was a hard and painful realization. As she was lying next to me one day, I wondered how I would be able to build a successful career, or even just go out again. Who would look after her if I got make-up jobs in other countries?

I could see I would have to turn down opportunities because I was needed by my dog.

There were so many instances that I wouldn't be able to take advantage of because I was held back in some way with the responsibilities of having a dog.

Looking back, I was a bit naive to think that having a dog would solve all the problems associated with my FASD.

A beautiful and loving dog like Barley, who had so much energy, needed a family that could give her attention 24/7. I have found it hard to write her name in this chapter up until now. Calling her 'the dog' makes the whole situation less personal, less painful.

Lovely Barley needed people to be around her who could go on tons of walks and keep up with her energy levels. She needed a family, not a two-person household. Luckily for us, we found her a great home with some friends. They also have a son with FASD and it's looking very hopeful that she will support him in the way she was supposed to support me.

There were tears when we said goodbye to her, but we know she has a much better life with her new family. We get regular updates from them, and she is having a great time.

While it's hard to write this, I am free in a way that I wasn't when I had Barley. I can hang out with friends and not worry about what time I get home. I can have a meltdown and not worry if it will stress Barley out. I can be my hundred per cent authentic self again. I can be lazy and have a bed day. I can go out all day and not worry about feeding the dog. I can go to jobs and not worry about a dog sitter.

Having a dog for six months definitely changed me. I understand now what it's like to have someone to look after. It's hard. Barley relied on me for basic needs, like food. It's a big responsibility, and it was so overwhelming that it made me depressed. I had no fun, as all my energy was drained.

But please believe me, when I tell you how lucky I was to have Barley, even for the short time I did. She taught me how to be a better human and I have a new profound respect for dog owners. For me, she was the right dog at the wrong time.

So, should you get a dog for yourself or your child with FASD?

Well, first, do not underestimate how much work is involved. It's definitely more than you think. You are responsible for a living being. Your life will change drastically, and you won't be able to do lots of things you did before you got a dog.

There will be lots of pressure, but lots of learning. If you are ready for that, it will be a hugely rewarding experience.

CHAPTER 24
The Rock: Anxiety and Low Mood

We often use the word 'rock' to demonstrate strength.

'You're my rock!'

'He's such a rock!'

Dwayne 'The Rock' Johnson.

I've heard people use the word 'brick' in a similar way, although I doubt Dwayne Johnson would enjoy being called 'The Brick'!

My rock is something very different. I wake up with this rock deep in my gut nearly every morning, and believe me, it's not a source of strength.

(Don't worry, this is not going to be a toilet story!)

I'm talking about my anxiety and my depression. They combine into a great stony bundle that I can actually feel inside me. A rock.

The thing about true depression is that it's not just mental, it's physical too. I feel this deep, deep sadness, this tiredness, inside my body. My Rock. I feel so heavy I can't move.

Sometimes I am fine, of course, but the most unexpected things can set off the depression, sadness and anxiety.

Being accepted onto *Glow Up* was one of the highlights of my life. Getting a 'Ding Dong' from the judges was off-the-scale wonderful. Getting a SECOND 'Ding Dong' resulted in floods of tears and me feeling as if my life was collapsing.

It makes no sense, does it?

As soon as I was told I had the second 'Ding Dong', I turned round and looked at the other make-up artists and I knew that they all hated me. But that was only true in my brain.

My anxiety was rising, and with it my depression. I went for a walk and cried and cried.

What was happening was that I was feeling sad for the others because they hadn't got a 'Ding Dong'. I was projecting onto them how I would have felt and getting sad on their behalf. It was all too much.

Afterwards, I spoke to the other contestants and cleared the air. I wanted them to understand not just how I was feeling, but why.

But the sadness, The Rock, remained.

I had the obvious solution; I would move into the house with the other make-up artists.

All the contestants were living in a huge house together, but Mum and I were in a hotel. It was definitely better that I had Mum beside me through this amazing, but often overwhelming, process.

Despite reservations on the part of the production team,

and huge worries from Mum, I insisted on moving into the house.

It was a very bad idea.

The minute I moved in, I was overcome with the sense that they all hated me. There I was again, projecting my feelings onto them once more. Whatever the reality of the situation, I didn't feel as if I belonged. They all sat in one room chatting, but I didn't join in. It was horrible to feel as if I wasn't wanted there.

The Rock was my only companion. Even Mum wasn't by my side to confide in. I phoned her at one o'clock in the morning. Talking to her helped me calm down enough to get some sleep.

The next day was devoted to practising our creative make-up looks for the next episode. I looked around at everyone else's work and was convinced mine wasn't good enough.

The next industry challenge was making up the performers in *Six: The Musical*. As a student of musical theatre, this should have been my challenge, the one I would triumph in.

After two days in the house, though, I was so depressed and overwhelmed, I couldn't even talk.

The Rock came with me, as I began work making up my actress. It wasn't my best work. I said so – on camera! Leaving the theatre, I felt so defeated and angry and carried this into the next day's filming.

I ended up in the Face-Off, where the two contestants who had done least well competed to stay in the competition. It was devastating. Drained, and sobbing in front of the cameras, I did my best. It wasn't good enough. I couldn't think straight, and my hands would not stop shaking. Remember the tremor in my right hand? Under duress it becomes worse. A make-up artist with a tremor! Go figure!

LIFE IN THE FASD LANE

I was eliminated. It was time for me to leave *Glow Up*.

Heading home, I was in such shock, I couldn't process what had happened.

I was so depressed, and, yes, traumatized, that I cut off from my creativity. I couldn't do make-up for ages.

The Rock and I huddled together in my bedroom.

Eventually, I emerged and I wrote this chapter. It was hard, but it has helped me to remember how much talent I have.

Soon, I want to start running my own make-up courses.

So, my friend, The Rock, I won't have time for you. Although I fear you may keep rumbling inside me.

You might say, 'But, Rossi, you've achieved so much, I can't believe you're depressed.'

Why, thank you. I have achieved a lot. I'm very proud of all I have done, but I have done it IN SPITE OF my depression and anxiety.

One thing I do know is that I will never apply for another television programme again.

Ooh, *Big Brother* is advertising for contestants...

CHAPTER 25

A Pinch of Salt

When I first tried SALT, I hated it. I thought it was a complete waste of time. But Mum thought it would help me to socialize and make friends at college. I decided to give it a try.

You thought I was talking about the white stuff you put on your fish and chips, didn't you?

No, I'm talking about speech and language therapy, usually shortened to SALT.

Although now I want some fish and chips!

As you know, I struggle greatly with social anxiety and knowing what to say and how to act in front of people. Even something as simple as forming a sentence can be a struggle for me, and more often than I'd like!

Part of the problem is that you might look at me and think, 'He's not disabled' or, 'He seems very friendly and open.' Then I'll say something highly inappropriate or hurtful and it looks as if I am just a nasty person. I'm not, of course.

But SALT helps me to focus not just on my words and manner of speech, but on my social interactions. The difference between my pre-SALT life and now is huge. I'm so grateful I was persuaded to go. I just wish I'd had access to this therapy when I was very young.

Back then, what little understanding I had of conversation came from the 1990s US TV show, *Charmed*. Spouting magic spells wasn't perhaps the most helpful way for a ten-year-old British boy to communicate. Maybe with some SALT I could have made proper friends.

When I was about eight or nine, I was in the local pub having lunch with Mum. As I walked to the pub's play area, I spotted someone I was sure I recognized from the telly. I introduced myself and asked, 'Are you so-and-so from that TV show?' She said yes, and I was so excited. My reply?

'Wow, you're so much skinnier in person!'

The lack of social filter that comes with my FASD meant that I was brave enough to approach a total stranger. But that same lack of social filter meant that I had no understanding that you simply can't say stuff like that.

Perhaps I can be excused because I was very young, but I was still doing this in my teens!

When I was in Year 10 at the BRIT School, the whole year group used to meet up in the canteen.

Everyone would be there, so I would just jump from group to group socializing, or what I thought was socializing! One fellow musical theatre student was a vegan, and I was eating bacon. It never occurred to me that I was actually making her feel sick.

I was 16 then, but mentally a lot younger.

I had SALT sessions throughout my college years and then more recently through my two years at Brushstroke Make up and Hair Academy. I've been doing these over Zoom every two weeks and I can see a big difference in the way I think about interactions.

A SALT session is a great way to unpick the week that has just gone by. All the social interactions I can remember, I talk about. I definitely have more confidence in my social life now.

SALT is daunting at first, but, like most things, you get used to it. Honestly, it was the best thing I could have ever done for my socialization skills. I really recommend it, but I do realize that it might not be appropriate for everyone.

Here's a really good example of how it's helped me. In one of my make-up classes there was a girl who I argued with, and my go-to riposte to her was, 'Money doesn't buy class. You may have money but that doesn't mean you aren't a chav!'

Harsh, right? I had become tired of her pretending to be better than everyone else. Naturally, I had offended her, and a few days later, I used what I had learned in SALT to resolve the issue. I took her to one side and said, 'I'm sorry for what I said. I was tired of what you were saying, and I acted out. I apologize.' She accepted my apology.

Solving the problem and apologizing is a major achievement for someone like me, and it's all down to more than a pinch of SALT.

CHAPTER 26

Global Developmental Delay

Yes, dear readers, it's time to learn a new phrase.

Global developmental delay.

What the heck is that?

So, here I am, aged 22, living my busy best life and thinking I'm SO independent and fabulous, able to build a house out of powder puffs and live in it like the queen I am! All sounds fab, right?

Then, it's hello, welcome to the real world.

I'm an adult but I get overexcited – a lot. The little seven-year-old Rossi inside me comes out for a while!

A 22-year-old man with the excitement of an infant school pupil. A grown-up behaving like a kid.

That's global developmental delay (GDD). My emotional and social development has yet to catch up with my physical age. It's delayed. Like a train that will come eventually, just not at the advertised time.

It's funny, though, because when I am with people older than me, I mirror their behaviours and seem very mature. My ability to hold a conversation is, if anything, ahead of my actual age.

GLOBAL DEVELOPMENTAL DELAY

But when I'm with younger people, I also mirror them. That feels easy and real for me.

I have a friend called Lici. She's seven years younger than I am but, somehow, because of this developmental delay I can relate to her.

We're like two little peas in a fabulous pod. We both struggle with impulse control and understanding time management. It's interesting to think of all the similarities we have, despite the age difference.

Of course, age really doesn't define a difficulty and when it starts and when it stops. For those of us living with FASD, these issues are lifelong. I am still learning how to live with them and work around them, to make adjustments.

But I am aware of my FASD all the time. It's a feeling of always being a bit out of sync with the world around me. Some things which should be easy can feel like climbing a mountain in ten-inch heels.

Whether it's trying to keep up with conversations, controlling my temper or making plans with friends, everything takes a little more effort and time, or some embarrassing learning curves.

Do you remember the story about the marble? The one I completely made up? Or maybe you haven't read that chapter yet, and I've spoiled the surprise.

Well, that was a great example of confabulation. I didn't intend to mislead you, lovely readers. I genuinely thought that it had happened. So, I told you the story because it was real in my head.

Confabulation.

All this confabulating is a good example of global

developmental delay. Seriously, which adult makes up stories like that? That's what little kids do.

Another side to confabulation is when I make up stuff on the spur of the moment, so I can join in the conversation. Or because I don't want to look silly. So, I say something to fill the gap. All eyes are on me. Yay! But also, aagh! Say something. Quick.

Recently, I was doing a make-up job for a film that was to be listed on an IMDB page. Ooo, get me! This is a big thing for any member of a film crew. If the film is listed, it means your name is on IMDB, and you can then have your own page on the site. Your own page on IMDB means potential employers can look you up. You have arrived, darling.

My mum came along to the shoot as she is currently also my PA until I can find one that can take her place. (She's irreplaceable, of course!)

She told me not to say she was my mum, but to tell the other people at the filming that she was just my PA. I was also to call her Jan.

Weird, eh? (Well, not so weird, because her name is Jan.)

She was trying to add a bit of professional polish to the situation. It really isn't the right vibe for the lead make-up artist on a film to have his mum there reminding him to do stuff. So, Jan it was. We'd already come this far, why not cosplay as a professional duo for the week!

Eventually she left the set, telling me to call her when I needed picking up.

The others all liked her and said how friendly she was, but wondered how and why I had a PA.

Now that is a super easy thing to explain, right?

Wrong!

GLOBAL DEVELOPMENTAL DELAY

I flap. My brain is yelling, 'Don't say she's your mum!' I have to say something, so down the confabulation rabbit hole I go.

'Well,' I say confidently, 'it turns out that Jan was the best of a bunch of people I interviewed for the job of PA.'

Of course I'm now enjoying this, I'm in the zone, and ten-year-old Rossi is embellishing this fabulous saga worthy of a Netflix mini-series. I continue.

'She might be old, but I felt she would have life experience and that would be a calming influence on a set, and she would be super trustworthy.'

Nobody even asked me that! It was all a load of made-up void fillers and funny backstory to build the character, darling!

I can't even remember the rest of the stuff I came out with, but I ended up calling Mum and telling her what had happened. She burst out laughing, calling me an idiot.

She barely talked to anyone when she came to pick me up for fear of finding out the other stuff I'd said but couldn't remember.

I'd got away with it. Well, I had, until the wrap party, when the lead actress and I got to talking about our mums' names! Turns out my mum and my PA are both called Jan, I told her! HAHA! 'Jan and Jan.'

Perhaps I shouldn't have invited this actress to my viewing party for episode one of *Glow Up*. My mum and my whole family would be there.

Eventually I confessed all to my actress friend. Thankfully she was cool about it. She told me she thought Jan was my mum anyway but didn't want to say anything and embarrass me.

So kind, but I felt foolish. I wish I could learn from this, but I know it will happen again. Hopefully it will happen less and less often, and slowly my developmental delay will catch up with me.

There'll be a few more embarrassing moments until then, to be sure.

It sucks to be honest, because with my impulsive nature, my keenness on people pleasing and my above average expressive language, it is a big ask.

I'm still aiming for my powder puff house, right!

An example of global developmental delay
This person is 18 years old, but their brain domains are at different developmental stages.

Age 18	Age 6	Age 12	Age 22	Age 8
Actual physical age	Attention	Academic skills	Expressive language	Executive functioning

GLOBAL DEVELOPMENTAL DELAY

Global developmental delay is when two or more of the brain domains have significant delays. For example, cognition and expressive language and adaptive behaviour. We went through these domains in an earlier chapter. Sometimes the terms 'developmental delay' and 'global developmental delay' are used interchangeably.

Sometimes, I just want to hide away, feeling as if I'm always one step behind. But with patience, understanding and the right support, I'm learning to navigate life in my own way, finding strength in the journey despite the challenges.

CHAPTER 27

Abstract Thinking

Mum said, 'Rossi, explain abstract thinking to your readers. You really struggle with it, and they might too.'

Thanks, Mum. Right, as always.

This is a very important topic. Abstract thinking has tripped me up a lot over the years. But what is it?

First, let's look at the word 'abstract'.

Something that is abstract is real, but it's not a physical object; you can't touch it. For example, love is real, but it's abstract. You can't pick it up or put it on a shelf at home. Money is not abstract. You can give me ten pounds. I have it in my hand. It's real.

Numbers, on the other hand, are abstract. You can't touch the number ten, unlike a ten-pound note.

The opposite of 'abstract' is 'concrete'; something you can hold and touch is concrete, solid. Much like our ten-pound note.

Back to primary school.

The whole class is standing in a field. We all have pencils and clipboards in our hands. We are about to try and solve a maths problem. Maths is abstract. It's numbers, you see.

ABSTRACT THINKING

All I want to do is strut across that grass like a model on a catwalk.

The teacher asks how far it is from here to the end of the field. How would I know? 'Guess,' she says. I can't do that. Give me a measuring tape.

Now I am being asked to draw the field on a piece of paper. How will that help? The paper is much smaller than the field. I can feel myself being overwhelmed by all of this. But apparently, it's easy. We'll do the calculations in our exercise books back in the classroom. How? The book is even smaller than the piece of paper.

If ever there was a time for my brain to be distracted, it is now. I can't fit a field in an exercise book. But isn't that girl's braided hair beautiful? I want to touch it. It's real, it's concrete.

The teacher comes and pulls me to the front of the classroom. She sees I am not writing in my book and is trying to explain the maths to me again. She is trying a different approach, but this is confusing me even more.

'*Pretend* the field can fit on the page. Better yet, forget the field and draw a line 10cm long.'

'Can I have a ruler?'

'No, you can guess.'

I am upset because I am at the front, next to the teacher's table and I can't see the girl's hair any more.

My mum noticed that I always cried on maths days. She told me not to worry and to do my best. I was only nine years old and feeling bad because I didn't 'get it', when it came to maths. Mum went to the school to discuss a solution. She offered to come in and do the maths lesson with me in a separate room.

Most kids would be horrified by having their mum take

them out for special lessons. Not me, I loved it. I felt very important. I was like Dr Who having my trusty assistant turn up just in time to evaporate maths. The relief of not always being the bad kid was immense.

Mum started working on how I could remember maths by finding physical objects to help me. I remember we used the floor tiles to learn what was a 'silly' *area*, including the 'nonsense' *perimeter*.

'Quick, run round the *perimeter*, a lion is coming! Now jump into the safe *area*.'

That's how I learned about surface area and perimeters.

Times tables were the best, as they involved us making up songs. I was good at songs.

3, 6, 9 – washing's on the line

12, 15, 18 – Louise has gone a-skating

To this day, I still can't do the three times table unless I use the song. But that's okay. I *can* do it, just in my own way. Poor Louise, though, she must be exhausted from all that skating!

This is how I learned maths, by making it silly. Maths is abstract and my brain can't grasp it in the same way most people's brains can. It's fine, I accept that. I accept that abstract things are weird. What's right here in front of me (computer, keyboard, screen, drink), that's what I need to deal with more urgently. I like living in the here and now.

Mum is still a big help. She deals with all the bank stuff. Yes, money is real, but not if it's just numbers on a screen. A plastic bank card is real, but how much is in my account? No idea as it is not physical. I could keep spending on my card, until the account is empty. But I get a thrill from shopping, that's what I mean about the 'here and now'. Right now, it's exciting to buy things, but whether there is any money for shopping, I don't really care.

Thankfully, I recognize this and my 'outside brain', that is, my mum, deals with all the money matters.

Timekeeping is another abstract concept. You can't see or touch two o'clock!

Mum oversees making sure I get to places on time. I know it's not good enough to turn up at two thirty for a two o'clock appointment, but I still do it.

Mum made me write this chapter. I'd much rather tell you funny stories. Some of them might even be true! But this, as she says, is important, and, as I read it back to myself, quite serious.

Perhaps you recognize your own behaviour, or the behaviour of someone you care for in this. You can't 'cure' a lack of abstract thinking overnight. The important thing is to find strategies to be able to deal with it. I have mine. What are yours?

CHAPTER 28

The Energy Bank

Every time I go to a shop and buy something with my card, my bank account empties by the amount of money that thing has cost me. One pound, five pounds, whatever the sum.

Every time I leave the house, go to college, or to meet someone, my energy 'account' also empties. Because of my FASD, my energy goes down very quickly, more quickly than my money!

I'm spending energy faster than I can earn it.

Being with people, in particular, drains my energy very quickly. This makes college or work a struggle.

In those people-heavy situations, I use a lot of my energy to appear neurotypical, to give the impression that I am the same as everyone else. That's known as 'masking'. It is like wearing a mask, so people can't see the real you.

As the day goes on, I am more likely to be a bit crabby and then I just want to get away from people.

When I get tired, I feel as if my body is shutting down. But it's my brain that drains even faster and more completely.

At the end of even a normal, stress-free day, it's not unusual for me to just crawl into my bed and watch television for several hours. By doing this, I am topping up my energy account, ready for the next day.

If I don't do this, my body and my brain will totally shut down. It doesn't happen often, but when it does, it's a kind of exhaustion that lasts for several days at a time.

If you need to spend time with me, be glad that I take this huge rest. When my energy is gone, I can't concentrate – sometimes I can't speak in full sentences! I get confused. With this comes a total lack of motivation. I don't actually want to do anything, go anywhere, or be with people.

And I might just be a bit grumpy.

I promise you I am not bored or lazy. I can't help it.

Mum talks about the brain fog that women of her age sometimes suffer from. Err, Mum, it's not only middle-aged ladies who get the fog!

What can be scary is that when my brain starts to shut down, so do my motor skills. My hands don't work properly any more. I literally can't pick things up or make a cup of tea.

So, how do I keep my energy account 'topped up' to a level where I am able to function well across the whole day?

Mainly, I am now much kinder to myself. It would be great if you could be kind to me, too. I know I need longer to formulate what I am going to say. I might take a bit more time to complete a task and I am learning to say no to activities or invitations, if I think they will drain me. I make a point of putting one day's space between major activities if I can and I don't take a job if it's straight after one I've just finished. If I don't do this, I get ill and will need to sleep for three days.

It's what I'd advise for you too, if you have FASD. Don't beat

LIFE IN THE FASD LANE

yourself up. Recognize your own energy bank levels and be clear about what you need. Never be afraid to say no.

For those of you who don't have FASD, please be patient with us. We'll get there.

And when we do, we'll still have some energy left in our account.

CHAPTER 29

My Fabulous Umbrella

I had a lovely weekend job at a garden centre.

One day, I was sent on an errand to a location on the other side of the gardens.

Picture the scene.

It is pouring with rain; I don't have a coat. Obviously, I need an umbrella! But I don't have one. Light bulb moment. I am in a shop that sells...umbrellas. I head to the umbrella display to pick out one I like.

That takes some time, but, excitingly, I find just the right umbrella. It looks stunning with the green tones of my uniform but gives a little flash of lemon zest to match the logo. Perfect, now I will look fabulous not getting wet.

I have not stolen the umbrella; I have

LIFE IN THE FASD LANE

borrowed it. There is a price tag clearly hanging off the umbrella, but this does not cross my mind.

I am hoping my employer congratulates me for taking the initiative.

Meanwhile, I am now late fulfilling my errand and all hell is breaking loose as colleagues are unaware of my rain dilemma. '*Where* is Rossi?'

Errand complete, the rain has stopped.

I ring Mum as it is lunchtime. I tell her that the manager is making a fuss because I took so long to do this errand and how I borrowed an umbrella.

Mum explains how you can't borrow umbrellas that are for sale, and that what I had done was wrong as it might look like stealing. Stealing! I am panicking. I am worried I will get fired. Or even worse, arrested! She tells me not to panic and to go and tell the supervisor who I get on with. So, I speak to my nice supervisor who, in turn, tells me to take the umbrella back and explain.

Simple, right?

No, not in my FASD world.

I return to the shop with the now contraband umbrella as quickly as I can. I head straight to the stand from where I had 'borrowed' it and, as I am trying to recall if it was next to the blue gentleman's golf umbrella or the multicoloured telescopic one I hear a voice asking, 'Where did you find that?' My FASD brain can't cope with the sudden intrusion into my thought processes. I didn't 'find' it. The question was wrong. What did Mum say? I can't recall, my thinking won't work. What did the nice supervisor tell me to say? I might say something wrong. I can't remember. My brain meltdown has stopped me from

MY FABULOUS UMBRELLA

verbalizing what had happened, and I just blurt out the first thing I can actually think of that fits her question, 'The staff room! I was told to bring it back here.'

I mean, why did I do that? I dug myself into a deeper hole than I was already in! I had told a lie I didn't need to tell.

I could not process, at speed, all the conversations I had had earlier with Mum and my nice supervisor, and this colleague, in front of me, needed an answer now! So, I said what I thought they wanted to hear because I could not remember what I had been told to say. I didn't 'find' it. I 'borrowed' it and all I can think is 'stealing' and I am scared.

My neurodivergent brain was trying to find solutions and really not coping well with that. I am not a thief, and I meant no harm.

Fortunately, I didn't get into lasting trouble, but it could have ended very badly for me.

Mum spends a lot of time explaining the difference between my 'reality' and what is real. But she can't be with me at work every day. That's why I need employers and colleagues to give me a bit of leeway, to understand that my brain is working differently, but that I am very capable.

Rossi's tip

If you ever find yourself in an umbrella dilemma or something similar, it's important to try and stick to the facts. It is easy to look back on these things and think, I should have done this, or I could have done that, but it is not quite so easy in the moment. Practise saying exactly what happened if you can remember it. But mostly, if you can't think straight, just say you don't know or you don't remember. When your brain has calmed down, you will be much better placed to explain, and a good employer will allow you that time.

If you are an employer and you know your employee is neurodivergent, think about how you approach a subject, and if you see them worrying, help them to finish their task and maybe have a catch up with them later.

This is easier for you and kinder on the neurodivergent employee.

CHAPTER 30

Hard Work

As you will have seen from that 'umbrella story', although I am still a student, I have been working part-time for a while now.

Let me tell you, work is hard.

Not the tasks themselves, I can do those. It's dealing with people, making decisions, and, most of all, taking instructions.

I'm not rude or arrogant; I don't mind taking instructions at all. It's just that, sometimes, I don't understand them. Or I think I have totally understood what my manager has said, and then I go and do something different – or just plain wrong.

Does this mean I can never have a job? Well, given that around half of disabled people don't have one, it doesn't look good for me, does it?

Getting a job is only part of the problem. It's keeping a job that can be tricky. Lots of disabled people find it hard and end up leaving their job because they find it too difficult to keep up. It happened to me!

In my last job in a make-up store that I loved, it was the rule that you could only leave the shop floor via a certain passageway, and NOT the front doors directly into the mall. My manager explained this to me. So far, so good. I understood, and when asking for a break she would often remind me by pointing her finger. When my manager was away one day, I totally forgot the rule and promptly got a warning for leaving via the front of the store. My colleagues reported me for blatantly ignoring the rules. Why did I do that on the day that the manager was not there? The manager was my memory trigger. Without her on the shop floor, my visual aid (her) was also not there. I was not thinking anything as I headed for my break. Seeing my manager was my reminder. With her absent, my brain didn't get the signal it needed to remember the rule. With her help, the shop put in place another way to remind me, but I left soon after. It was too difficult for me, and it was very frustrating repeatedly getting things wrong.

Of course, that doesn't happen to everyone. There are very understanding employers out there, and to be fair, the shop management did try to help.

I know I have skills and talents, and I want to use them for good. What I, and other people with FASD, need is understanding from our would-be employers. Just by making a few changes, you can enable our best work and benefit yourselves in the process.

Now, that's a win-win!

Top of the list is communication.

I'm very good at communicating in the sense that I talk fluently – and often! But I'm not great at expressing what I need when I am right there, in the middle of a situation.

Remember the lie I told about where I got the umbrella? It's just one example.

If I don't understand, I'll probably nod my head in

agreement. Then I'll try to figure it out for myself and hope you'll congratulate me.

Tips for managers

To all my future managers, here's what would make my working life smoother, and would help you to get the best out of me.

The best me means you get the best work I can do.

Perhaps you could create guidelines like this for yourself and your particular needs. A good employer will be happy to receive this information.

HOW TO COMMUNICATE WITH ME AT WORK

My name is Rossi.

I have FASD, which affects how my brain processes information. If you give me too much information, and in a complicated way, I can become overwhelmed.

It's really helpful if you communicate with me in the following ways:

- Give information in one or two sentences maximum, if possible.
- Use clear, simple language.
- Speak in the positive (e.g. say, 'Please do this', rather than, 'Please don't do that').
- Avoid the use of acronyms and jargon (e.g. don't say, 'EOD', say, 'end of day').
- Speak calmly and slowly in a clear voice.
- Ask me if I have understood what you just said.

LIFE IN THE FASD LANE

- Check that I have understood, because, at first, I might just mumble that I do understand, when actually I don't.
- Repeat the information, either in the same words, or in simpler words.
- Ask me again if I have understood. I *promise* it's not patronizing if you have to ask several times, as long as I have understood.
- Once you know me, try to speak to me in the kind of words you know I would use.
- Adopt a relaxed posture. (If you look stressed, I will sense that and feel stressed too.)
- Understand that if I do make a mistake, I mean no harm. I am neurodivergent; I won't always get it right!
- Above all, please be *patient* with me.

Thank you for supporting me in doing my best work.

CHAPTER 31

Alcohol and Me

Alcohol – wine, beer, gin and so on – is such a huge part of British life. We drink it at every celebration. We drink to relax. A pub is where we often meet our friends.

I say 'we', but I really mean 'people other than me', because I have a difficult relationship with alcohol.

It's alcohol that caused all the physical and mental challenges I deal with every day. I'm not blaming my mum in any way. She was just doing what everyone does, having drinks with friends. She didn't know that little Rossi was inside her, being harmed by those drinks.

As a British teenager, I too wanted to have a social drink, to be like everyone else. But what baffled me was why I couldn't just go out, drink beer and get absolutely trashed like everyone else my age.

The problem for me is that the getting trashed bit comes way too easily. If I drink even a small amount of alcohol, I feel the effects for the next week. At least, it feels like that.

Having FASD means that alcohol just doesn't seem to sit within my body the same way it does with other people. It's been quite the journey to find this out!

My first memory of drinking alcohol goes back to when I was five and at my sister's 18th birthday party. It was fancy dress, and everyone was dolled up to the nines. I was obviously SLAYING in a full Edwardian suit, frills and all. I looked fabulous and felt very grown up.

This frilly-shirted mini-adult took a huge, not-so-grown-up swig from a fancy glass of sparkling apple juice. And then spat it right back out again. Of course, it wasn't juice, it was champagne, as any real adult would have known.

It was the perfect drink for a birthday party, but not for a five-year-old, frills or no frills.

When we lived in Norwich, Mum would occasionally go out to the pub and take me with her. She would drink with my dad or her friends, sometimes beer, sometimes wine, and I was fascinated by these coloured liquids that they all seemed to like so much.

I would have a pint of lemonade with a straw because I thought that looked cool. I knew that one day I would drink beer and wine just like Mum and her mates, and I knew they would be as sweet and tasty as my lemonade.

And so there I was at the party, spitting out champagne and wondering why adults all chose to drink something so gross.

Years later, my London college crew would go out and get sloshed/trashed/wasted. The common thing was to go to house parties and drink cider. I was partial to the fruit cider, Kopparberg. DELISH! Sweet and fizzy, a bit like my lemonade from years before. But I never liked the way I would feel at the end of the night. Groggy, dizzy, and with swollen hands.

I would never really get hung over in the traditional way. Even when I drank a lot, I would emerge the next day with a bad stomach, dizziness and sweaty, swollen hands. My body was telling me very loudly not to drink alcohol, thank you very much.

It took a good while and multiple conversations with Mum to really understand the danger alcohol can cause to my system. Too much alcohol is dangerous for anyone, but more so for me, as I already deal with several physical challenges, thanks to FASD.

I also understand that having FASD makes me more inclined to addictive behaviour. Addiction is a slippery slope. It can ruin addicts' lives, as well as the lives of those who love them.

In many ways, I am grateful that my body says, 'No! Don't go there!' Nobody wants swollen hands for days!

Now, I don't drink alcohol at all. It's better that way.

I can't tell anyone else what life choices to make, but I feel very strongly that if there is a danger you might become addicted to anything (alcohol, drugs), just say NO!

It might feel odd, and your friends might try and persuade you to have 'just the one' or call you boring. Social pressure is horrible! But a swift 'No, thank you, I don't drink alcohol', can save you from those swollen hands or whatever specific thing happens to *your* body after drinking.

Your friends might ask you to explain why you don't drink. You don't have to tell them. But, if it increases their understanding, it might be a good idea to tell them why.

Then enjoy a lovely glass of juice or 0 per cent alcohol drink, socializing and *no* awful side effects.

CHAPTER 32

Mum's Eye View

Jan, Rossi's mum

Rossi has been known to describe our house as manic.

I thought he was talking about somebody else's house. As a family, we lived a very quiet life. Rossi's life, on the other hand, now that was manic!

He would come home from school, run upstairs and transform into his alter-ego, Jamie Elia. Jamie would spend hours making music videos and posting them on social media. Rossi lived in Jamie's world. It was a world he had created to help him cope with the real world, one in which he didn't fit. It was also a world he could control. He likes to be in control.

There was that time, one September, when I started getting calls from parents about when to drop their kids off for Rossi's birthday party. He'd invited the whole class. His birthday is in February! Those invitations were a way to both take control and to try and form bonds with his classmates.

It's interesting to look back and see that he thought the manic-ness extended to me and his brother and sister. Only, what he sees as reality, and what is real, are not the same thing at all.

As a parent, one of my roles is to be Rossi's 'outside brain'. Some *people might be offended by that term, but it's the phrase we have always used. It's a role I'm happy to take on because Rossi's 'inside brain' can get so muddled.*

We've had other people fill the role too, like his teaching assistant. Rossi needs discipline and structure. But I am, for now, the chief 'outside brain'.

I would say I'm quite an old-fashioned parent. Not strict, but I am very strong on discipline and structure.

Many children with FASD are adopted, but I gave birth to Rossi. It is unusual for a birth parent to talk so openly about their experience, but I think it's essential. I want to remove the stigma and shame around FASD, especially for birth mothers.

I went through menopause at the age of only 36. I already had two children and was told I couldn't have any more. It never occurred to me when I was having a drink down the pub that I might be pregnant.

I do ask myself a lot of 'What if' questions.

'What if I hadn't had that beer?'

'What if I had known I was pregnant?'

'What if I had known the damage alcohol could do?'

That's the hidden side of having a child with FASD, thinking about what might have been. It's a rabbit hole I do gaze down sometimes, but then swiftly turn away from. It's painful.

As my mother's generation used to say, 'If ifs and ands were pots and pans, there'd be no need for tinkers.' Those 'What ifs' can fill every corner of your life.

Rossi has already told you that he had numerous 'symptoms' as a youngster, yet nobody could diagnose what it really meant when you put all these symptoms together. So, I did what any of us would do, I googled them. The first thing that popped up on my screen was

LIFE IN THE FASD LANE

Surrey FASD clinic. On their website was the story of a young man called Andrew. As I read his symptoms and his challenges, whenever his name appeared on screen, in my head it was replaced by 'Rossi'.

This was my son's life I was reading about! Here, at last, was an explanation, a diagnosis, though not yet an official one.

There was also the realization that I was responsible for Rossi's struggles. I had consumed alcohol and, as a result, my son was disabled. It was a horrible way to find out, but it was a moment of clarity. Now I understood 'why'.

I had spent many a school pick-up hiding behind a tree, dreading the moment the teacher would seek me out to complain about Rossi's disruptive behaviour. Equipped with my new understanding, I could now take control of the situation and get Rossi an official diagnosis.

He was finally diagnosed with FASD when he was 12.

It might seem to outsiders that I'm something of a helicopter parent, always hovering over Rossi. But, in addition to being Rossi's outside brain, I need to ensure his safety, and support him through his anxiety and depression, so he can do all the things he loves.

If you saw him on *Glow Up*, you might be surprised to read that Rossi suffers from anxiety. On television, you saw him brimming with confidence, especially in the early stages of the competition. What you didn't see was the deep inner conflict that went on before the cameras rolled. It would shock you to see it. Of course, lots of creative people have anxiety, and it can be what drives them. But Rossi has it ten times more than most.

That is the real story of someone living with FASD.

The only place Rossi is really Rossi is at home with us. Happily, that's beginning to change as he learns about his condition and accepts help.

He has big ambitions for himself. To achieve these, he needs to be able to navigate the world safely. I am confident he will achieve his goals, but his timeline will be different from most other people's. With each passing year, I see him growing in wisdom and experience, all of which makes him that bit safer.

He is 22 now but in some aspects of development he is still like a three-year-old. In other areas he's like a 16-year-old. Those areas of development vary hugely across young people with FASD. Some of those living with FASD have IQs below 70, classing them as cognitively disabled. However, a lot have IQs in the low average to high range.

Where it becomes difficult is when the levels of understanding vary within one person. For example, Rossi's ability to hold a conversation exceeds his understanding of instructions. But because he talks so fluently, people assume he knows more than he does. This can lead to huge problems in seemingly everyday situations, at school or work. This is why he needs my ongoing support.

Most youngsters of his age are aching to get away from their parents, but Rossi's showing no signs of wanting to leave home. As long as he wants to stay, that's fine with me. There's no rush.

We're getting him a part-time personal assistant, someone else to be his 'outside brain' for a while, who can help him organize the chaos that his life can be. For example, he needs help with travelling and understanding money. Honestly, he'd spend everything he has on non-alcoholic champagne and smoked salmon. He is very aspirational and doesn't understand money or budgeting or delayed gratification. He wants it all NOW, even if he can't afford it. Every morning, we look out of the window to check if the money tree has sprouted five-pound notes. So far, nothing, but I remain hopeful!

My lasting wish is that Rossi meets someone who loves him the way I do. I hope that person is willing to go the extra mile and take on the role of the 'outside brain'. It's a role that is easier if there's love involved. I won't always be around. But as long as I am, I'll be here to support him.

I am so proud of my son for creating this book. I am proud to be a part of it.

As I have often said, as parents and carers of young people with FASD, we need to focus on what they are good at. Their gifts. Rossi is a fantastic make-up artist, and now he's a writer. I might, of course, be just a teeny bit biased, but by shining a light on what a young person can do, we build their confidence. We stop them being another person who fails in a school system designed for neurotypical children.

It's important to get the full story of living a life with FASD out into the wider world. I wish I'd had someone to give me the benefit of their parenting experience. I hope my experience, and Rossi's story, will benefit other parents.

CHAPTER 33

What Can We Do to Stop FASD?

Now you know a little bit more about what life is like for someone living with FASD.

But what next?

I'm so happy that more is being done in the medical world, and by society at large, to help people like me.

A lot of very clever groups of people have made in-depth studies of the condition – universities all over the world and groups of researchers. Some governments fund the research.

A recent study suggested that, across the world, 630,000 children are born every year with the condition. It has now been shown that 2.5 times more children are born with FASD than are born with autism, Down syndrome and cerebral palsy combined. These figures are mind-blowing.

The study also found that FASD wasn't about whether you were rich or poor. It can affect everyone.

We've heard the word 'pandemic' a lot in recent years. I really feel like this is another pandemic. If it is, don't we need a vaccine of some kind?

Of course, you can't inject women with something that will

stop them drinking alcohol during pregnancy. But FASD is entirely preventable. It doesn't need to exist at all.

Women need to *choose* not to drink when they are pregnant or think they might be. To make the right choice, they need the right information. So, we need to get the facts out there. This book is part of that process, I am happy to say. My appearance on *Glow Up* also gave me a chance to talk about FASD to a national television audience.

Knowledge leads to understanding, which I hope will lead to a change in attitudes to alcohol and pregnancy. I know if my mum had been given the facts, she would have made a choice which would have given us both a different life.

When she gives talks and presentations, she always says, 'If I knew then what I know now.'

Think about how much drinking alcohol is a part of our culture. We meet friends in the pub, we have a drink. We go to a restaurant; we order a bottle of wine with our meal. We toast our birthdays with champagne. There's nothing wrong with that. But, if you are pregnant, think you might be, or are trying for a baby, you have to say no to that drink.

There are loads of non-alcoholic drinks available now. You don't just have to have a lemonade. There's alcohol-free beer, wine and gin!

I know it's hard. Your friends will say, 'Oh, come on. Just the one won't do any harm.' I'm afraid that even one drink really could cause your baby harm.

There are now even UK Government guidelines[1] on drinking during pregnancy. What do they say? Don't drink! There is no safe amount.

---

1   NICE Quality Standards Code of Practice

WHAT CAN WE DO TO STOP FASD?

Don't drink and carry a child in your womb!

I am not a scientist and, of course, I don't want anyone to think I am lecturing all women of child-bearing age. I also want you to know that I am happy with my life. But, as you have read, my life is filled with challenges that affect me and the people who love me. How much smoother daily living would be for all of us without those challenges.

Mum and I are often asked to give presentations on what it is like living with FASD, on our lived experience. We have done webinars for doctors and midwives and have made videos for training sessions. It is something we are passionate about.

Not because we want to bash women who drink when pregnant, but because we don't want mums to feel bad because they didn't know.

Mum said that when she found out that I had FASD, she had a choice between feeling sad and guilty, or using her experience to change people's understanding.

We are friends with lots of adoptive parents and foster carers who took on children not knowing the difficulties that lay ahead for them. We explain to them that the birth mum did not do this on purpose. She didn't know the damage alcohol could cause. Even if she was addicted to alcohol, she certainly didn't intend to hurt her child.

I have done lots of shows for FASD advocates, and I have spoken and sung at Wembley for Voice in a Million and Adoption UK. Fifteen thousand young people learned about FASD that night! If we can change one unborn baby's future, then that's a good thing.

CHAPTER 34

Finding Our Brilliant

All of us have a gift, a talent. Maybe more than one. Nearly all of us, I believe, have a passion.

I am very lucky in that my gift and my passion are the same – make-up.

In 2024, my love of make-up, and my commitment to it, led me, as you know, to the BBC series, *Glow Up*.

But that love all began much earlier.

I can picture myself, as a little boy, stealing my sister Jodie's make-up. Of course, I thought I was just borrowing it.

I gave myself a fabulous blue undereye with bright pink lid shadow and BRIGHT RED lipstick. Can you imagine it? I was clearly going for the abstract avant-garde look. It's the kind of thing they would have loved on *Glow Up*. I have always adored playing with colour and texture.

Years later, I went to school to learn about make-up. The classroom has always been an uncomfortable place for me, even when I was following my passion.

I always found it hard to listen in class or follow the pace and speed at which the lessons were taught. Happily, I did

136

qualify as a make-up artist, and now I'm learning again, this time about hair. It's not easy, but my passion keeps me going.

What I wish, more than anything, is that a make-up course existed that catered to people like me, people whose disabilities make learning a struggle. I wonder who might be a good person to start a class like that?

Surely, it's ME!

For the longest time I've wanted to teach others with learning difficulties and physical disabilities how to become successful make-up artists. Nobody should be held back from pursuing their dream career. We need a place where disabled people can learn the skills to become a success story in their own right!

Creativity is essential to our well-being. Everyone deserves the chance to create, no matter what difficulties they face. The beauty world needs to work harder to foster inclusivity and promote self-esteem, so that talented disabled people can make a career in the industry.

But the beauty industry has a wider social responsibility as it has the power to show the world that beauty comes in many forms and knows no bounds. It is making good strides in representing the diversity of its customers in its advertising, but there's still a long way to go.

I would love to be a voice for those often ignored by an industry that likes to show us what the 'ideal' person should look like.

It's also really important that beauty professionals should receive training on how to work with neurodivergent and disabled clients to make them feel welcome.

LIFE IN THE FASD LANE

My friend Lici, who is only 12, sings at Wembley every year! She has the most amazing voice. She can riff and write lyrics and deliver a powerful vocal in front of 15,000 people. But like me, she struggles with numbers and writing and social skills! Her mum helped her to shine! She is learning the piano now so when she is older she can maybe be a teacher.

Another young man I've known for a long time is Tolka. He loves to be called TB. He struggles even more than I do in social situations, and he also has trouble with numbers and with being independent. But oh my goodness, what he can't do on a computer and mixing desk! He is such a great singer songwriter producer. He has had his music played on the radio! How? He has a family who support him. They enable him to do the thing he can shine at. Brilliant? Yes, he is.

These are just a couple of examples of people I personally know with FASD who have found their brilliant, as we call it. There are so many more.

I really want to be a voice for disability awareness in my world, the beauty world. I want the industry to empower everyone to feel confident and beautiful, whatever their daily challenges. A whole world of confident, beautiful people. Shouldn't we all want that?

CHAPTER 35

The Real Rossi - At Last

It's been quite emotional recounting many of my personal experiences for this book. I should be used to talking about myself by now. It's been my privilege to give talks to lots of people with FASD and their families, and to others in the FASD community.

Two huge gifts have come from meeting so many people with FASD. The first is the wonderful feeling of knowing I am not alone. The second is the realization that, although each person with FASD is different, we are all very connected.

Remember at the beginning of the book, I mentioned the 420-plus conditions that might affect us? Each of us has our own mix of those conditions that we deal with every day.

And yet, we have one huge thing in common – we struggle to find our true voice. I know I'm not the only person who has difficulties being 'real' in social situations.

I've spent so much time trying to please people, I've often left my own personality on the back burner. I focused my energies on creating a character that my fellow students or work colleagues would find likeable.

People-pleasing is exhausting.

I am much better now at reminding myself that my true personality and my values are important. I tell myself that I am not alone. I tell myself I am strong. Every day I deal with something very difficult, and from that comes my strength.

I know now that I must take the time to adjust to each new situation. Not rushing allows my brain to grow comfortable with people, places, information.

Part of growing up has been realizing my limits and adapting in order to live with FASD, instead of fighting against it, or pretending it isn't there. I spent too long doing that.

Does it seem strange to read that? You know I'm a person who loves the limelight and is happy to give talks and discuss my condition quite openly. Behind the scenes, I have always been scared of accepting my FASD, as if doing so would make me less of a person. As if I would be seen as weak and not as good as everyone else around me.

To be honest, I still struggle with this.

This is why this book is so important to me. My goal was to show all the ups and downs of the FASD life, and how, even if you understand that life well, it will always throw challenges at you. But with support and understanding, we can all reach our full potential.

If you picked up this book thinking it would show a path to the perfect way of living with FASD, I think you will have been disappointed. There is no 'perfect'.

The invisible nature of FASD still leads to misdiagnosis. Can you believe that? Doctors know so much more than when I was born, but some kids are still not being diagnosed quickly enough. That's so sad, because they'll be going through what

I went through ten or more years ago. They'll be seen as the disruptive ones, the difficult ones. They'll be the targets for bullies.

Happily, we are going in the right direction. More people know about FASD than before, and I hope this book plays a big part in spreading the word even further.

Everybody has a beautiful gift to give the world. As my wonderful, supportive mum always says – Find Your Brilliant.

I am a brilliant make-up artist. There, I said it.

It doesn't mean I don't go through 'stuff'. Even now I sometimes find myself falling asleep in class. My brain and body are drained of energy and off I snooze. I worry the teacher will think I am disrespectful.

There are days I desperately wish I was 'normal'. But, hey, what is normal anyway? Everybody is dealing with some kind of 'stuff'. It just so happens that mine is FASD.

Do you know what that makes me? A

F abulous
A nd
S assy
D iva!

(Do you see what I did there? FASD!)

Get out there and be Fabulous too.

An Editor's Tale

Hello.

My name is Mel Byron. Who? I'm new to you, but I've been here all the time. I've been an invisible presence, but definitely here.

I am what is known as a Development Editor, and I've been working with Rossi to turn his stories into this book. The Development Editor does lots of things, from correcting grammar, to helping turn a lot of disconnected thoughts into individual chapters that flow well, and that will be informative and entertaining for the reader.

Rossi and Jan were keen that I shared some of my own experiences of working on Rossi's World. It's been very different from other projects I have worked on, because it's the first time I have worked with a writer with FASD.

What's important is that you, the reader, understand that Rossi didn't just sit down at a computer and produce thousands of words. That's not, as I have learned, how the FASD brain works. Sometimes even getting a few hundred words from Rossi

AN EDITOR'S TALE

for me to work on has been challenging. Emails, WhatsApp messages, meetings, missed meetings, Zooms. And still no new chapters. Then suddenly, a whole flurry of chapters because Rossi is 'in the zone'.

There have been times when he has started to tell a story verbally that I had no idea about, so I have scribbled furiously to capture it, in case he didn't write it down himself.

You could say I have been an honorary, temporary 'outside brain'. I've been the chaser, reminding him and his mum of deadlines, work to be done.

When the material has come, I've looked at what Rossi has created and applied my expertise to make it shine. To use his words, to make it 'fabulous, darling!'

We haven't always agreed. Or Rossi and I agree, but Jan doesn't. Or Jan and I agree, and Rossi thinks I am totally in the wrong. There have been 'discussions' about tiny details. What to me seem like key topics we need to decide on have been seen as trivial. A case of 'Whatever!'

I've had to learn to be very patient. One thing it took me a while to understand is that Rossi's mind is full of contradictions. We've had meetings where Rossi was very animated, then would suddenly just get up and walk away.

At one meeting he told me the book was finished and had been submitted to the publisher. That's confabulation at work, right there! I can tell you that, as I write this, it has not been submitted! But in Rossi's mind, the job was done.

Writing a book is hard, and I know that for him it's been, at times, overwhelming.

But I admire Rossi's determination and his unshaking belief

that his story will be of help to so many other young people and their families. The process of getting his story written has not been easy, but it has been necessary.

Helping to write this book has been an education for me. Reading this book will be an education for so many more.